Best Practices from America's Middle Schools

Charles R. Watson

James Madison University
Harrisonburg, VA

EYE ON EDUCATION

EYE ON EDUCATION
6 DEPOT WAY WEST, SUITE 106
LARCHMONT, NY 10538
(914) 833–0551
(914) 833–0761 fax

Library of Congress Cataloging-in-Publication Data

Watson, Charles R. (Charles Ray), 1944-
    Best practices from America's middle schools / Charles R. Watson.
        p.   cm.
    Includes index.
    ISBN 1-883001-66-8
    1. Middle school teaching--United States.   2. School improvement
programs--United States.   3. Middle school education--United States.
4. Educational change--United States.   I. Title.
    LB1735.5.W38   1999
    373.73--dc21

98-31707
CIP

10 9 8 7 6 5 4 3 2

Editorial and production services provided by Richard H. Adin
Freelance Editorial Services, 9 Orchard Drive, Gardiner, NY 12525
(914-883-5884)

Also Available from Eye On Education

Middle School Block Scheduling
by Michael Rettig and Robert Lynn Canady

Teaching in the Block: Strategies for Engaging Active Learners
by Robert Lynn Canady and Michael Rettig

Teaching Mathematics in the Block
by Susan Gilkey and Carla Hunt

Teaching Foreign Languages in the Block
by Deborah Blaz

Supporting Students with Learning Needs in the Block
by Marcia Conti-D'Antonio, Robert Bertrando, and Joanne Eisenberger

The Interdisciplinary Curriculum
by Arthur K. Ellis and Carol J. Stuen

A Collection of Performance Tasks and Rubrics: Middle School Mathematics
by Charlotte Danielson

**Performance Assessment and Standards-based Curricula:
The Achievement Cycle**
by Allan Glatthorn, with Don Bragaw, Karen Dawkins, and John Parker

**The Performance Assessment Handbook
Volume 1, Portfolios and Socratic Seminars**
by Bil Johnson

**The Performance Assessment Handbook
Volume 2, Performances and Exhibitions**
by Bil Johnson

Instruction and the Learning Environment
by James Keefe and John Jenkins

The Paideia Classroom: Teaching for Understanding
by Terry Roberts with Laura Billings

The Educator's Brief Guide to the Internet and World Wide Web
by Eugene F. Provenzo, Jr.

Research on Educational Innovations, 2d ed.
by Arthur Ellis and Jeffrey Fouts

Research on School Restructuring
by Arthur Ellis and Jeffrey Fouts

Data Analysis for Comprehensive Schoolwide Improvement
by Victoria L. Bernhardt

The School Portfolio
by Victoria L. Bernhardt

Transforming Schools into Community Learning Centers
by Steve R. Parson

Educational Technology: Best Practices from America's Schools, 2d ed.
by William C. Bozeman

The Administrator's Guide to School Community Relations
by George E. Pawlas

**The Reflective Supervisor:
A Practical Guide for Educators**
by Ray Calabrese and Sally Zepeda

The Principal's Edge
by Jack McCall

The Principal as Steward
by Jack McCall

Preface

Since the early 1960s, middle-level schools have been consistently and continually working to improve the ways that the pre- and early adolescent child is taught. Middle schools were among the first schools in the country to use flexible block schedules, giving more time and more flexibility to teachers and teams. Middle schools pioneered the use of interdisciplinary teams as instructional structures, and teams continue to be one of the foundational aspects of middle level education. Middle schools also took some of the better ideas generated in the "open education" days and improved them, adapted them, implemented them, and evaluated them. For example, during the days of open education (and I am old enough to remember those days) thematic instruction was often mentioned as a way to improve a child's understanding of conceptual materials and content. Middle school teachers and curriculum developers have taken this idea and in many, many locations have stretched and adapted the idea into rigorous, conceptually sound, and relevant units of study that help middle school students make sense of what are often very complex and abstract ideas and concepts.

Because of their dynamic environments and energetic atmospheres, middle schools were also among the first schools to experiment with different forms of governance, even before the current "site-based management" approach was in vogue. Team leaders, exploratory teachers, parents, counselors, and administrators often become the team that makes the decisions for a school.

Middle schools also were among the first to create and adopt methods to help students understand this unique period of life. Teacher-advisory programs do not replace good middle school counselors, but they provide at least one other person to whom a child can go for assistance, support, and advocacy. Advisory teachers are also often the primary contact for parents of middle level youngsters.

There is no dearth of innovative, creative, and unique programs in middle schools. Like all schools, however, change and improvement efforts must be responsive to a multitude of forces that seem to be constantly at work in school communities. That is, regardless of the innovative program or approach, school improvement is always difficult and is always subject to scrutiny. And many of these innovative programs and approaches simply haven't worked; after many years of studying the phenomenon we call "school change," we know some of the reasons why some programs work and others don't. Michael Fullan (1993),

v

perhaps the leading authority on school change, suggested that we really don't need more innovation, we need to look at the problems of school improvement through a different lens or with a new mindset. Looking carefully at the innovative approaches included in this book demonstrates that in most of the programs, the people involved in developing and implementing an innovation are doing just that—using a new lens to look at a problem and its solution.

I began this book as a result of my work as a middle school teacher and now as a middle school-teacher educator. As a public school teacher, I was regularly subjected to reforms, programs, and improvement plans, most of which arose from somewhere outside of my school. As I mentioned, I began my teaching career during the days of open education, and for many years I struggled with ways to make the ideas inherent in open education work—often to no avail. As my career progressed and my experience and skills as a teacher grew and improved, it appeared to me that many of the school-reform programs and innovative strategies attempted at my schools had about the same life span as a mayfly. Many of you recognize effective schools, mastery learning, project learning, quality circles, SRA kits, Distar, and other programs; now we have outcome-based education, total quality education, Basic Schools, Accelerated Schools, Success For All, Core Curriculum Model, and others. The difference, as I see it, is that in the early years, little or no real evaluation or assessment of the programs took place. After all, we aren't allowed to fail in our efforts, for that would mean we have somehow failed the children and parents who were subjected to these efforts. Therefore, it is my opinion that many of these earlier programs, if they were evaluated at all, simply created preferred results in order to sell themselves to an interested public. That isn't so true anymore. Most of the innovative programs are being extensively evaluated on a number of variables and in a number of ways; we are finally looking at results, although in many cases our examination of results have come about as a result of legislative action or pressures to be accountable. But we are beginning to see results that are truly positive and impressive.

As a teacher educator, I spend a lot of time in schools, often working with students and practicing teachers as they go through the business of teaching. What I have found in my work with schools around the country is that we are still looking for programs that can become our panacea—we are still looking for that program, or method, or strategy that will solve our problems. But I am also finding that there are some differences from my earlier experiences. I am now seeing many more programs, projects, and strategies being created, coordinated, managed, and evaluated by teachers and administrators at the school level. I am also seeing teachers in the unique professional role of researcher —teachers are becoming much more active in terms of systematic inquiry into practice and programs.

The programs in this book are, for the most part, those that originated at the school level and which were adapted or implemented by teachers, parents, and principals who are closest to the problems the programs address. In addition, nearly all of the programs have undergone assessment and evaluation based on the desired goals of the program. And in most cases, the same professionals are doing the evaluations; after all, it is their world, their students, and their children who are affected. This is different from my early experiences as a public school teacher. I can't recall ever having been asked to systematically evaluate any of the reform efforts or programs in which I was involved. If an evaluation took place at all, it originated outside of the school, and regardless of our professional opinions about a program, the program always seemed to work.

I used a number of sources and criterion for selecting a program. The four major sources were national and regional middle-level conferences, the Internet, the ERIC database, and recommendations from practitioners. The criteria I used for selection were fairly broad, but all selections had to have direct influence on practicing teachers and principals, had to have distinct goals that were related to students, and had to have results. For some of you the programs may not appear to be very innovative or creative; but as I travel around the country looking at schools, I often find that what is a common practice or approach in one area of the country is completely unknown in another.

Finally, there are several common threads that are found in most, if not all, of the programs, without which most of these programs would not have been successful. First, in nearly all of the cases, the programs were initiated by groups of professionals representing all levels of interest; that is, very few, if any, of the programs were mandated from outside the school community. Yet, those who developed and implemented the programs were clearly focused on being accountable for their actions. Second, in nearly all of the cases, the programs are viewed as "in progress." You will sense, as I did, that whatever the program, there is a very real feeling that the program will probably never be complete or finished.

How the Book is Organized

The book is organized into five broad chapters with subsections in each chapter. In Chapter 1, Part 1 includes several wonderful programs that address the very real need of parents and children to make a successful and safe transition from elementary school to middle school. Part 2 includes strategies and programs that describe different approaches to interdisciplinary teams, perhaps the most important aspect of making the transition from elementary to middle schools effective and successful.

Chapter 2 is divided into three parts that deal with curriculum, instruction, and assessment. In Part 1, there are a number of creative curricular programs that have had success. Part 2 shows that instruction can take many unique and creative forms, including the use of technology and creative ways to group students. Part 3 presents programs that help teachers and parents more accurately assess and evaluate how well students have mastered the curriculum, and some strategies that teacher and students can use to reflect on their progress.

Chapter 3 is a broadly defined chapter; that is, I have included a number of programs and approaches that range from student health to student recognition; from at-risk students to alternative schools; and from violence prevention to community involvement. Also included are extracurricular or intramural programs, and there are successful advisory programs, one of the most difficult aspects of middle-level education to implement. But in all cases, the focus is on student support—addressing the needs of children to keep them engaged in school and learning.

Chapter 4 looks at programs that address the very real need for schools to broaden their communities and involve those in the school community with student success. In Part 1, there are successful parent programs. In Parts 2 and 3, there are successful programs that widen the community's commitment to the children in our schools and challenge us to address the needs of children beyond the walls of the school building.

Finally, Chapter 5 takes a look at several programs related to the professional development of teachers—both pre-service and in-service teachers. The need for bright, dedicated, enthusiastic, and motivated teachers is great and will become greater, and the need for teachers who love teaching in middle schools is even greater.

How to Use This Book

This book can be used in several ways, and the following suggestions are simply the limits of what my imagination can produce. I am sure others will find more ways to use the book. But my purpose in writing the book had less to do with generating a list of possible programs than it had to do with showing teachers, principals, other administrators, parents, and students, that there are many, many ways to improve what is done in middle schools to better address the needs of middle-school students. My central purpose is to help you think about these programs and how they might apply to your schools, and to encourage you to borrow the ideas presented and adapt them to your individual needs and situation. That is one way to use the book: look at the programs presented here, think about how the programs might be suitable for a school, perhaps call or e-mail the contact person, and then begin the process of making your middle school more successful. For your convenience, a matrix of programs and middle level issues is included on pages x–xv. I have included it because most of the programs in this book actually address a number of related issues found in middle schools. You may use the matrix, for example, if you are looking for programs that deal with parental involvement, just find the topic on the vertical axis and look across at the various programs that include this topic.

Another way to use the book is to use it as a reference or guide to show others that creative approaches can and do work. The book might be a way to confront the "been there, done that" attitude that often prevents us from moving forward.

Acknowledgments

There are many people who have been extremely helpful with this project. But there are four who provided the most assistance: First is my wife Lucy, who didn't miss a day asking me how the project was going and who allowed me to ruin many pretty weekends to work on the book. I also want to acknowledge Temple Aylor, Sarah Jarvis, and Jacqueline Beliveau who organized many of the programs, searched the Internet, read drafts of the manuscript, and otherwise helped me put things together.

I would also like to thank all of the dedicated, creative, and motivated teachers and principals who submitted programs. I realize how busy you all are and I appreciate the time you took to describe your programs. Finally, to all the middle-school students I have taught and those I haven't, thanks for being the wonderful children you are. I pray you will have nothing but the best of teachers in the best of schools.

Reference

Fullan, M. (1993). *Change Forces*. New York: Falmer Press.

	Salt Lake City, p. 7	Shuksan Middle, p. 10	Stonewall Jackson, p. 237	Gavit Middle, p. 17	Highlands Middle, p. 21	Smith Middle, p. 27	Ormand Stone Middle, p. 34	Angola Middle, p. 37	Taylor Middle, p. 40	Rochambeau Middle, p. 49
Transitions	◆	◆	◆	◆	◆	◆				
Peer Helping	◆	◆	◆	◆	◆					
Team Structure						◆	◆	◆	◆	
Team Roles							◆	◆	◆	◆
Multigrade Teams						◆				
Literacy Skills										◆
Literacy Curriculum										◆
Science Processes										
Science Content										
Interdisciplinary Instruction		◆				◆		◆	◆	
The Arts						◆				◆
Student Motivation, Behavior	◆	◆	◆	◆	◆				◆	
Student Research										◆
Student Technology Use		◆	◆							
Portfolios										
At-risk Students	◆					◆	◆		◆	
Student Health Welfare						◆	◆		◆	
Student Recognition										
Sexual Harassment										
Conflict Resolution									◆	
Alternative Programs						◆				
Intramural Programs										
Advisory Development										
Parent Involvement	◆		◆		◆	◆				
Volunteers			◆							
Community Communication				◆						
Community Service				◆			◆			
Teacher Education			◆							
Professional Development			◆							

	Willis Middle, p. 52	FAST Program, p. 55	Radnor Middle, p. 59	Black River Middle, p. 64	William H. English Middle, p. 67	Hines Middle, p. 70	Clark-Pleasant Middle, p. 74	Roosevelt Magnet, p. 79	Wayland Middle, p. 82	Eastwood Middle, p. 85
Transitions										
Peer Helping										
Team Structure										
Team Roles										
Multigrade Teams										
Literacy Skills			♦	♦	♦	♦		♦		♦
Literacy Curriculum			♦	♦	♦	♦		♦		♦
Science Processes	♦	♦	♦				♦			
Science Content	♦	♦	♦				♦			
Interdisciplinary Instruction	♦	♦	♦		♦	♦	♦		♦	
The Arts		♦	♦							
Student Motivation, Behavior		♦		♦		♦	♦	♦	♦	
Student Research			♦			♦	♦			♦
Student Technology Use			♦	♦						♦
Portfolios										
At-risk Students					♦	♦	♦	♦	♦	
Student Health Welfare								♦		
Student Recognition						♦			♦	
Sexual Harassment										
Conflict Resolution										
Alternative Programs										
Intramural Programs										
Advisory Development										
Parent Involvement	♦								♦	
Volunteers									♦	
Community Communication	♦				♦				♦	
Community Service	♦				♦				♦	
Teacher Education										
Professional Development										

	Hightower Trail Middle, p. 89	Mandeville Middle, p. 92	Institute for School innovation, p. 96	Mount View Middle, p. 101	Lawrence Middle, p.104	Scott Middle, p. 107	Charlotte Day, p. 110	Lake Braddock Secondary, p. 113	Roosevelt Middle, p. 123	Spratley Middle, p. 125
Transitions										
Peer Helping										
Team Structure						♦				
Team Roles										
Multigrade Teams						♦				
Literacy Skills			♦	♦			♦	♦		
Literacy Curriculum			♦					♦		
Science Processes	♦		♦				♦			
Science Content	♦						♦			
Interdisciplinary Instruction	♦	♦				♦		♦		♦
The Arts			♦							
Student Motivation, Behavior	♦	♦	♦	♦			♦		♦	♦
Student Research				♦				♦		
Student Technology Use	♦	♦				♦		♦		♦
Portfolios			♦	♦		♦				
At-risk Students		♦							♦	
Student Health Welfare		♦					♦		♦	
Student Recognition							♦			♦
Sexual Harassment										
Conflict Resolution										
Alternative Programs									♦	
Intramural Programs										
Advisory Development										
Parent Involvement									♦	
Volunteers										
Community Communication		♦							♦	
Community Service									♦	♦
Teacher Education										
Professional Development										

	Challenger Middle, p. 129	Guilford Middle, p. 132	Knox Middle, p. 136	Neumann School, p. 139	Washington Irving Middle, p. 141	Ellicott Mills, p. 145	Stewart Middle, p. 149	George Washington Carver, p. 152	Best Foundation, p. 155	Macario Garcia Middle, p. 161
Transitions										
Peer Helping										
Team Structure						♦				
Team Roles			♦			♦				
Multigrade Teams										
Literacy Skills			♦	♦						
Literacy Curriculum			♦	♦						
Science Processes										
Science Content										
Interdisciplinary Instruction		♦		♦	♦		♦			
The Arts										
Student Motivation, Behavior	♦	♦		♦	♦	♦	♦	♦	♦	♦
Student Research										
Student Technology Use										
Portfolios										
At-risk Students		♦		♦		♦		♦	♦	
Student Health Welfare		♦		♦		♦		♦	♦	♦
Student Recognition										
Sexual Harassment	♦									
Conflict Resolution			♦		♦					
Alternative Programs		♦		♦			♦	♦		
Intramural Programs										
Advisory Development										
Parent Involvement								♦		
Volunteers								♦		
Community Communication							♦	♦		
Community Service							♦	♦		
Teacher Education										
Professional Development										

	Murphysboro Middle, p. 164	Hilltonia Middle, p. 167	Geneva Middle, p. 170	ASPIRA, p. 173	Goochland Middle, p. 179	Bernardsville Middle, p. 182	Wallace Middle, p. 185	Aylor Middle, p. 188	Lake Oswego Junior High, p. 197	Peabody College, p. 200
Transitions										
Peer Helping										
Team Structure										
Team Roles										
Multigrade Teams										
Literacy Skills										
Literacy Curriculum										
Science Processes										
Science Content										
Interdisciplinary Instruction										
The Arts										
Student Motivation, Behavior		♦								
Student Research										
Student Technology Use										
Portfolios										
At-risk Students	♦	♦	♦							
Student Health Welfare	♦		♦		♦	♦	♦	♦		
Student Recognition										
Sexual Harassment										
Conflict Resolution						♦				
Alternative Programs		♦								
Intramural Programs										
Advisory Development			♦	♦	♦	♦	♦	♦		
Parent Involvement									♦	♦
Volunteers									♦	
Community Communication				♦					♦	♦
Community Service								♦	♦	
Teacher Education										
Professional Development				♦	♦	♦	♦			

	Sarah Scott Middle, p. 206	NY City Middle Schools, p. 213	Trent Lott Middle, p. 216	Georgetown Day, p. 221	Frederick County, p. 224	Lake Taylor Middle, p. 227	Western Middle, p. 240	Frost Middle, p. 244
Transitions								
Peer Helping								
Team Structure							♦	
Team Roles								♦
Multigrade Teams								
Literacy Skills								
Literacy								
Science Processes		♦	♦					
Science Content		♦	♦					
Interdisciplinary Instruction		♦	♦	♦				
The Arts								
Student Motivation, Behavior	♦		♦		♦	♦		
Student Research		♦						
Student Technology Use		♦						
Portfolios								
At-risk Students	♦				♦			
Student Health Welfare					♦	♦		
Student Recognition								
Sexual Harassment								
Conflict Resolution						♦		
Alternative Programs	♦	♦				♦		
Intramural Programs								
Advisory Development								
Parent Involvement	♦					♦		
Volunteers		♦	♦	♦	♦	♦		
Community Communication	♦	♦	♦	♦	♦	♦		
Community Service	♦	♦	♦	♦	♦			
Teacher Education								
Professional Development							♦	♦

About the Author

Charles R. Watson has been working in middle schools for over 25 years as a teacher, an administrator, a counselor, and a teacher educator. He is currently an Associate Professor of Education at James Madison University where he teaches, writes, and does research in middle education, curriculum articulation, science education, school change, and teacher leadership. Currently the Executive Director of the Virginia Middle School Association, he has served as a consultant to over 100 schools and school districts, and has given presentations at over 50 national and state conferences. Dr. Watson can be reached at James Madison University, School of Education, Harrisonburg, Virginia, or via e-mail at watsoncr@jmu.edu.

Table of Contents

If...

your middle school has successfully implemented a program or project which ought to be considered for the planned next edition of this publication, please contact us:

Eye On Education
6 Depot Way West
Larchmont, NY 10538
(914) 833-0551 phone
(914) 833-0761 fax
e-mail: middle@eyeoneducation.com

1

Transitions and Teams

By its very nature, the middle school period of a child's life is transitional. It is during this period of life that some of the most important human transitions take place. Children's bodies are beginning to change in ways that are frightening and dramatic: their minds are expanding, they are intensely curious, and they are beginning to think abstractly; they are facing choices that we often find hard to imagine as we reflect on our own lives; and they are moving from the warm and caring elementary school environment to what they may mistakenly perceive to be the hard and cold middle school environment.

Children, as are their parents, are often afraid of this transition. Children are afraid of lockers, changing clothes for gym class, not making friends, moving between classes throughout the day, finding the library, being around eighth graders, and getting on the right bus. To a large extent parents are afraid of these same things, although perhaps for different reasons; and, of course, the move from elementary school to the middle school seems to happen just about the same time that many adults also find themselves in transition.

The cornerstone of most middle schools is the idea that we can use teams to provide some semblance of order and belonging for children and parents. Interdisciplinary teams provide subject-matter expertise, an ability to transform content into meaningful, integrated, and relevant lessons and activities, and the notion that the size of the school matters less than how teams operate and define themselves.

This chapter is divided into two parts: The first deals with the unique and perhaps most frightening transition for students and parents, from the elementary setting to the middle school setting, and the second part deals with innovative team structures and goals. The first part has several programs that schools have designed to make this transition easier and more effective for both students and parents. In all cases, the programs are taken seriously and implemented with care and good planning. The programs, in many cases, have parents playing important roles in making the transition easier and more acceptable to other parents.

In the second part, the teams and team structures vary widely and the approaches to interdisciplinary teaching and learning take many forms. This form of teacher assignment brings about new and different roles for teachers while it adds to teachers' professional responsibilities.

Transitions: Elementary to Middle

These programs demonstrate how schools have made the transition from elementary to middle school easier and more effective. In several of these programs, parents play important roles in making the transition more acceptable to other parents.

Bridging Elementary and Middle School Efforts to Facilitate At-risk Students During Transition: Salt Lake City Schools (Utah)

> Total districtwide process that involves meetings between schools and teachers on a regular basis; elementary instruction incorporates middle school issues and problems

FAST—Fifth and Sixth Together: Shuksan Middle (Washington)

> Program that uses mentors, e-mail pen pals, and cross-school interdisciplinary thematic instruction to bridge gaps between middle and feeder schools

A Comprehensive Orientation Program: Stonewall Jackson Middle (Virginia)

> Parents are used as speakers and orientation mentors to assist students and parents new to the middle school

Big Brother/Big Sister 6th Grade Orientation Program: Gavit Middle (Indiana)

> Big Brothers/Big Sisters mentoring model that uses school visits, student communication, and guest speakers

Transition to the Middle: A Workable Plan: Highlands Middle (Kentucky)

> Extensive details and communications about students between feeder and middle school teachers and the use of many student-led activities both before and after the transition

Bridging Elementary and Middle School Efforts to Facilitate At-risk Students During Transition

Salt Lake City School District, Salt Lake City, Utah

This large-scale, innovative transition program is unique, especially with respect to the extent elementary teachers and staff work, including using instructional strategies, to help students, especially those identified as at-risk, move from elementary schools to middle schools.

The Program's Goals

♦ To assist students, especially those identified as at-risk, from 13 feeder schools make a smooth and academically sound transition to the middle school, and to actively involve teachers, parents, administrators, and counselors in the efforts.

How the Program Works

♦ During the first year, teachers from both the elementary feeder schools and the middle school met once a month from January through April to share ideas, work together, and build trust. During those meetings, presentations and workshops were given on such topics as "at-risk" students, preadolescence, self-esteem, and the purpose of making effective transitions.

♦ Information fairs are now held each spring at each of the feeder elementary schools, during which parents visit booths staffed by teachers, administrators, and counselors from the middle school.

♦ Instruction at each of the elementary schools incorporates and integrates "life in the middle school" into various lessons. For example, elementary mathematics lessons may include demonstrations about combination locks, geography lessons may include maps and routes to the middle school, and language arts lessons may include aspects of surviving in the middle school. In addition, middle school students write letters to the elementary students about "succeeding" in the middle school.

♦ Elementary students spend a "transition day" at the middle school where they:

- Attend and visit classes;

- Attend an assembly;

- Are given tours of the school.

♦ In the fall, all entering students are enrolled in a comprehensive outdoor education program that is designed to build:

- Goal setting;

- Acceptable social risk-taking behaviors;

- Team building;

- Trust in themselves and others.

How the Program is Funded and How Much It Costs

♦ The program received a $1500 grant to pay for the initial planning. The elementary schools pay for substitute costs and transportation costs for the "transition day" activities. Students from the local university also volunteer as substitutes for the elementary teachers to attend the various activities.

Things to Consider

♦ Due to its extensive nature and the involvement of many schools, it is important that the program be managed and facilitated by a single person. This person needs to be able to communicate well with both teachers and parents and to motivate teachers to participate, as well as know how to build collaboration.

Current Progress and Results

♦ The program has been in effect for five years and is quite successful. In addition to increased teacher morale, better parent relations, and improved communication among schools, the middle school students have experienced improved grade-point averages, fewer absences, and improved citizenship grades.

School and Demographic Information

Clayton Middle School
1471 S. 1800 East
Salt Lake City, UT 84108

♦ 730 students, grades 7–8; 40 teachers; 28% free/reduced lunch; 80% white, 20% minority; small urban.

Contact

Joanne S. Brunetti
3521 Suniland Drive
Salt Lake City, UT 84109
Voice: 801-481-4806
Fax: 801-481-4924
E-mail: stevane.godina@slc.k12.ut.us

FAST—Fifth and Sixth Together

Shuksan Middle School, Bellingham, Washington

This very innovative, year-long program combines a number of curricular and transitional elements into a unique method for linking fifth grade elementary school children with students in the middle school, making the transition to middle school easier as well as allowing students from both schools to contribute to a service-learning project and to engage in rich interdisciplinary learning.

The Program's Goals

- ◆ To aid in the transition from elementary to middle school.

- ◆ To provide a needed service to the community.

- ◆ To engage students in an interdisciplinary, curriculum-based project.

How the Program Works

- ◆ At the beginning of each school year, fifth graders from feeder elementary schools are paired with sixth graders in the middle school. These pairs become e-mail pen pals and communicate regularly throughout the year.

- ◆ Teachers from the various schools are also teamed as partners or team-teaching pairs and work together throughout the year on the projects and programs.

- ◆ Teachers at all schools choose a comprehensive, interdisciplinary project (ecological- or environmental-based) that has a strong service-learning component to bridge learning activities among the schools.

- ◆ Students from both the elementary schools and the middle school participate in joint learning activities and events as the unit progresses. For example, students participate together in project presentations, tours of a conservation site, salmon releases, stream restoration projects, tree plantings, and classroom visits.

♦ The focus of the thematic approach combines academic work with real-life problem-solving that contributes to a larger community benefit.

♦ Students also engage in reflective writing that places personal value on the activities, as well as allows the teachers an opportunity to assess activities and understanding.

♦ Students give presentations regarding their individual and collective work and conservation efforts using multimedia presentation programs that are presented to groups at all schools.

How the Program is Funded and How Much It Costs

♦ The program is funded both locally and through external grants. Shuksan Middle School teachers wrote and were awarded a grant from the Learn and Serve America Foundation, and support also came from the local Americorps group, which provided stipends for coordinators of the program.

♦ The grants supported teacher training, snacks, an instructional assistant, substitutes for teacher curriculum planning and development, and evaluation.

♦ Additional assistance comes from local university students and faculty.

Things to Consider

♦ As a complex and comprehensive program, teacher training and planning are critical and it is suggested that at least one year be devoted to planning.

♦ A shared vision is also critical. It is suggested that teachers, administrators, parents, and students collaborate to develop a clearly defined vision statement that incorporates goals for school improvement, student learning, and faculty development.

- The choice of a locally important theme is essential. The theme should be meaningful for students as well as the parents and other adults involved in the project, and it should be one that has social and community value. Successful completion of a project should contribute to the overall community welfare.

- The curricular and instructional aspects of the thematic unit take a great deal of time and effort on the part of teachers. Adequate time and financial support should be given to the teachers prior to implementation as well as during the program.

- The complexity of such a program demands that a project coordinator be used to facilitate and manage the various aspects of planning and coordinating the year-long process.

Current Progress and Results

- The success of the program at one middle school compelled the school district to implement the program at its remaining middle schools and their respective feeder elementary schools.

- The principal of the middle school reports dramatically fewer discipline problems both in classrooms and during lunch.

- Parents of new middle school students report fewer transitional problems for their children as they move to the middle school and they are quite happy about the program.

- The school has received numerous forms of recognition and positive publicity from the community and the media.

- Teachers report that many pen pal relationships continue throughout the grades and cross-grade communication has improved.

- The focus on the curricular aspects of the thematic approach help elementary and new middle school students gain better understanding of the differences between elementary and middle academic subjects and expectations.

- Teachers and parents report that the students appear to have stronger self-concept and higher self-esteem as a result of the year-long program.

School and Demographic Information

Shuksan Middle School
2713 Alderwood Ave.
Bellingham, WA 98255-1298

◆ 530+ students, grades 6–8; 31 teachers; lower/middle class: 40% free/reduced lunch; 80% white; small urban.

Contact

John Andes
Shuksan Middle School
2713 Alderwood Ave.
Bellingham, WA 98225
Voice: 360-676-6454
E-mail: jandes@sms.bham.wednet.edu
Web Page: http://www.sms.bham.wednet.edu

A Comprehensive Orientation Program

Stonewall Jackson Middle School, Mechanicsville, Virginia

The manner in which this middle school uses parents as a key part of its orientation program is unique. Parents are used as speakers to introduce new parents to the school, as hosts for a fall open house, and to assist new middle school parents with parenting issues. Another unique element of this program is the use of "shadowing for a day" as a way to introduce students to the school.

The Program's Goals

◆ To share information about the middle school with new parents and new students.

◆ To reduce fears about coming to the middle school for students and parents.

◆ To improve academic performance and success with positive, emotionally and physically safe climates and environments.

How the Program Works

◆ In January of each year, the teacher leader for each grade level and the principal of the school conduct an assembly with the fifth grade elementary students and teachers at each feeder school. The assembly points out the similarities and differences between elementary and middle schools, including the way the schedule works, what clubs and sports are available, and how the locker system works. A lengthy question and answer session is also planned for this assembly.

◆ During this assembly, the counselors from each school (elementary and middle) meet to discuss transitional issues and ways to alleviate fears and prevent problems from occurring. Following the assembly, counselors from the middle school meet with each fifth grade class to describe students' elective options as well as answer additional questions.

- Soon after the January assembly in the elementary schools, an introductory meeting is held for all of the fifth grade parents whose children will be moving to the middle school. A parent of a current sixth grader and a current sixth grade student from the middle school are among the speakers, and provide information and advice as to how best to prepare for the transition. New families are also given the opportunity to purchase items with the middle school's logo.

- Later in the spring, all fifth grade students visit the middle school for a tour and see performances given by student groups; several sixth grade students give welcoming speeches and advice as well as answer student questions.

- Near the end of the school year, two additional important events take place. First, a representative from each fifth grade class from the feeder schools is paired with a sixth grade student; the fifth grade student "shadows" the sixth grader throughout the day, then reports back to his or her respective fifth grade class. Second, the parents conduct a "Parent-to-Parent" Open House for parents of fifth graders where the central topic is about parenting a middle school student.

- Copies of the final middle school newsletter are mailed to all parents of fifth graders with a welcome message and other news about the school.

- Each family or parent is also provided with the telephone number of another middle school parent to call for help or questions. Networking among parents is strongly encouraged, both formally and informally.

- In August, a fairly traditional open house is conducted, when parents can meet teachers, have schedules explained, walk through a student's scheduled day, practice opening lockers, and so forth. Parents and students are also given copies of the school's handbook.

- Several other methods for introducing the parents and students to the school are also used, including distributing course syllabi for each class, introducing media and technology, holding a "Back-to-School" evening meeting and open house conducted by the P.T.A.

How the Program is Funded and How Much It Costs

- Costs are minimal, rarely more than $100 per year; the costs, however, in terms of time and effort are substantial.

Things to Consider

- Survey parents of fifth graders prior to the initial events to determine the main concerns held by the parents.

- Provide various opportunities for parents to learn about the middle school without becoming overwhelmed by too much information.

Current Progress and Results

- Parent support is extremely high and continues through all grades, as parents become mentors and partners with the upcoming fifth grade students' parents. Academic achievement is improving as students know that their parents are supportive of the schools, its teachers, and its administration.

- Relationships among the middle and elementary schools and teachers have improved a great deal.

School and Demographic Information

Stonewall Jackson Middle School
8021 Lee-Davis Road
Mechanicsville, VA 23111

- 1200+ students, grades 6–8; 90 staff; 92% white; suburban.

Contact

Dr. W.A. Valentino or Joni S. Pritchard
8021 Lee-Davis Road
Mechanicsville, VA 23111
Voice: 804-730-3307
Fax: 804-730-3231
E-mail: wvalentino@hanover.k12.va.us
Web Page: http://www.hanover.k12.va.us/sjms/sjmindex.html

Big Brother/Big Sister Sixth Grade Orientation Program

Gavit Middle School, Hammond, Indiana

This highly effective transition program combines four methods of easing the transition of fifth graders into the middle school. The key to these methods is the use of student mentors, or "Big Brothers" and "Big Sisters." The use of these student mentors helps new middle school students overcome many of the more frightening aspects of the move from an elementary to a middle school.

The Program's Goals

The program's goals are divided into two categories. The first category of goals is to provide support to the incoming sixth grade students, and the second goals category is to provide a social growth benefit and opportunity to current sixth grade students.

- ◆ To support fifth grade students, including establishing a strong link between Gavit Middle and the seven schools that feed into Gavit.

- ◆ To provide an ongoing connection between Gavit and the elementary schools.

- ◆ To provide an opportunity for fifth grade students to discuss their concerns about going to the middle school with peers who have "survived" the experience.

- ◆ To introduce incoming fifth grade students to the ideas of community and team spirit.

- ◆ To provide an opportunity for current sixth grade students to participate in a community outreach program, assume leadership roles and responsibilities, and practice interpersonal communication skills.

How the Program Works

- The Big Brothers/Big Sisters program is actually the culminating part of Gavit's orientation program. The orientation program includes visits to the elementary schools by the principal, assistant principal, and the counselor, each of whom participate in programs for the fifth grade students who will move to the middle school the next year. These visits take place about midway through the second semester.

- In early May, all seven of the feeder elementary schools send their respective students for a half-day onsite visit. During the visit, fifth grade students tour the school and participate in several activities and programs designed to introduce the middle school programs and structures to the new students.

- In mid-May, the sixth grade's Big Brothers and Big Sisters visit each of the elementary schools and through a set of structured and scheduled activities, talk with the students in both formal and informal ways to allow for more personal interaction and allow the new students the opportunity to discuss their concerns with the Big Brothers and Big Sisters.

- A few days before the first day of school in August, the Big Brothers and Big Sisters meet with the administrative team and are given instructions and schedules regarding their responsibilities and duties on the first day of school.

- On the first day of school, Big Brothers and Big Sisters provide assistance to the new students with directions, provide assistance with lockers and lock combinations, and assistance with lunchroom arrangements. Big Brothers and Big Sisters are excused from class on the first day of school.

How the Program is Funded and How Much It Costs

- Basic expenditures are minimal, although initially, Gavit was provided with grant funds from the Lilly Endowment in Indianapolis. Currently, costs include funds to purchase Big Brothers/Big Sisters T-shirts for the team of 30 students, and substitute pay for the three teachers who accompany three groups of ten students to the seven elementary schools the students visit.

Things to Consider

♦ It is very important that each school's schedule be accommodated and planned well.

♦ The selection of appropriate students is critical to the success of the program. Gavit looks for a relatively homogeneous group of students that represent the demographics of the school population. It looks for solid, average students who will be credible to the fifth grade students; some students who have had minor behavioral difficulties are included to portray a "been there, done that, don't want to do it again" attitude toward discipline.

♦ Securing the support of the sixth and seventh grade teachers is also crucial. It is also wise to send many thank you notes after the program is completed, including notes to the feeder schools' teachers and administrators.

Current Progress and Results

♦ The program has been in place for five years. Many eighth grade students, who are going on to the high school, mention that being a Big Brother or Big Sister was a high point of their tenure at the middle school.

♦ Many parents write testimonial letters and statements regarding their support for the program and their desire for it to continue.

♦ The incoming fifth graders indicate higher levels of comfort entering the school and that getting down to the business of school is much easier.

♦ Sixth grade Big Brothers and Big Sisters indicate that they feel more self-confident and poised, as well as more responsible and able to communicate.

School and Demographic Information

Gavit Middle School
1670 175th Street
Hammond, IN 46324

♦ 630 middle school students (1550 total middle/high population), grades 6–8; 84 teachers; very diverse; 30% free and reduced lunch; urban.

Contact

Elaine Pitts
424 W. Deerpath Drive
Schererville, IN 46375
Voice: 219-864-9360 (h); 219-989-7325 (s)
Fax: 219-864-0121

Transition to the Middle School: A Workable Plan

Highlands Middle School, Ft. Thomas, Kentucky

The innovative aspects of Highland's transition program are its depth, breadth, and the extent to which student leaders are involved. The program begins in the early spring and is completed only after the students have made the transition to the middle school in October.

The Program's Goals

- ◆ Successful transition of elementary school students to the middle school

How the Program Works

- ◆ In March, the sixth grade teachers (elementary) meet with the seventh grade teacher teams (substitutes provided) to discuss:
  - Special education students, including Individualized Education Plans (IEPs);
  - At-risk students;
  - Special student assignments (who should not be placed with whom, personalities, behavior, etc.);
  - Medical and other concerns or issues.
- ◆ In March, all sixth grade teachers complete a recommendation form for each student moving to seventh grade that includes performance levels in all subjects, general abilities, and teacher comments.
- ◆ In April and May, the middle school counselor and special education teachers meet with all sixth grade (elementary) special education students.

- In April and May, assistant principal and counselor hold orientation meetings with parents of all sixth grade students.

- In May, all sixth grade students attend a half-day orientation at the middle school where these types of activities take place:

  - Middle school student leaders guide students in a poster-creating activity that is designed to introduce each student's unique talents, characteristics, and abilities;

  - Middle school student leaders lead students in "getting-to-know-you" activities;

  - Middle school student leaders answer questions about middle school life;

  - New students are given a tour of the building.

- In early August, before the start of school, sixth grade students are given the opportunity to attend a summer "Transitions" class led by middle-school student-leaders during which new students:

  - Are given practice with locks and lockers;

  - Are exposed to the various class and course schedules, including lunch and bell schedules;

  - Are given another tour of the building with special attention paid to specific rooms;

  - Are given a typical "supply list;"

  - Are given copies and explanations of schools rules;

  - Take part in simulations of problems student may face during the first days of school (e.g., losing a schedule, not finding new friends, forgotten locker combinations, meeting new students, getting lost in the building, etc.).

- In early September, the assistant principal and counselor hold additional meetings for all parents new to the school.

- In early October, student leaders and new students participate in a "Big Brother/Big Sister" program.

How the Program is Funded and How Much It Costs

♦ The program is funded through local allocations; additional costs for substitute teachers are also paid by local funds.

Things to Consider

♦ The program is very time-intensive for teachers, counselors, administrators, and students; care should be taken to provide school staff the time they need to plan the various events as well as to accommodate for student leaders' involvement.

Current Progress and Results

♦ Students and parents are very comfortable with the transition to the middle school. Teachers are especially grateful for the additional student information they receive and have been able to make accommodations and adjustments based on their knowledge about the new students, especially with respect to behavioral expectations.

School and Demographic Information

Highlands Middle School
2400 Memorial Parkway
Fort Thomas, KY 41075

♦ 400+ students, grades 7–12; 30 teachers; less than 3% free/reduced lunch; small suburban.

Contact

Diana Myers McGhee
3407 Heathermoor Blvd.
Taylor Mill, KY 41015
Voice: 606-782-3333 ext. 28
Fax: 606-441-9371

Teams: Making the Difference for Students

In these programs, schools take different approaches to teams, team structures, and interdisciplinary teaching and learning:

Multigrade Teams: Smith Middle School and Bead Middle School (Florida)

> Multigrade grouping and team assignments, extensive assessments, and continual parent communication across two schools

Reaching for the Stars: Ormond Stone Middle School (Virginia)

> Organization and assignments of roles and responsibilities make this team's approach to interdisciplinary arrangements effective

Who Needs a Principal? The Team Can Do It All!: Angola Middle (Indiana)

> Very effective, autonomous team combines service learning, extensive and effective communication, school-community relations, and a focus on academics

It's Our School!: Taylor Middle (California)

> Strong focus on school community and academic climate, emphasis on teacher decision-making and responsibility, and continual assessment of progress

Multigrade Teams

Smith Middle School, Bead Middle School, Florida

These two different middle schools' approaches to interdisciplinary teaming and instruction are based on grouping sixth, seventh, and eighth grade students on individual teams. That is, each team contains students from all three grades. This innovative approach is discussed a great deal in educational circles, but is rarely implemented effectively. Therefore, the descriptions of this important innovation are longer than others in this book and contain additional details regarding implementing this approach.

The Programs' Goals

- ◆ Improve academic performance and effective education.
- ◆ Improve sense of family and community within teams.
- ◆ Improve interpersonal relationships within teams.
- ◆ Demonstrate that multigrade teams can work as effectively as traditional grouping arrangements.
- ◆ Improve students' transition from elementary school to middle school.

How the Programs Work

- ◆ At **Smith Middle School**, parents opt to place their children on the multigrade team that is composed of about 120 students of varying abilities. The Loggerhead team has 60 gifted students, 10 students with identified learning disabilities, and 50 who are classified as "regular" students. The five teachers on the team were assigned to the team based on experience and licensure, and little additional training was given. No waivers or exceptions were given from the state regarding this team.
- ◆ The Loggerhead team focused on developing a three-year sequence of comprehensive interdisciplinary units of study and used assigned

textbooks primarily as resource materials. The interdisciplinary units of study allowed for differentiation within the unit to address the wide variance in abilities and talents.

◆ The Loggerhead team used a variety of assessment strategies to determine student learning and plans. Portfolios, performances, and oral presentations complemented traditional tests, quizzes, book reports, and written papers, giving the team a wider view of individual student success and needs.

◆ At Smith Middle, and particularly on the Loggerhead Team, several structural and instructional barriers were successfully overcome. Textbooks, as both supplemental and primary texts, needed to be available for all three grade levels on the team. Sixth graders experienced additional anxiety entering the team as they were concerned about older students and how the older students would accept them. Some students, especially the seventh and eighth grade students, expressed concern about being segregated from friends who were in traditionally graded classes.

◆ At **Bead Middle School**, the school population is much more diverse and the multigrade team, the 6-teacher Piranha team, was composed of 110 students from middle and lower income families, over 25% of whom qualified for free or reduced lunch. The Piranha team served gifted, regular education, and special education students, and much effort was given to insuring that the team population accurately mirrored the school population. Teachers for the Piranha team were chosen for their knowledge of content, their use of innovative teaching strategies, and their communication skills.

◆ At Bead Middle, parents had a choice as to whether their child was included on the multigrade team, and although there was some initial negative response, informational meetings with parents overcame the objections and built a base of strong parental support.

◆ Piranha teachers also implemented a number of thematic, interdisciplinary units of study, which allowed them to vary the level of expectations and assignments based on individual student skills, abilities, and handicap. The level of cooperation and sharing among students were greatly improved and enhanced by thematic instruction.

◆ Piranha teachers also used a number of assessment procedures that more accurately reflected student understanding and achievement, including traditional forms of testing and evaluation as well as more authentic strategies.

How the Programs are Funded and How Much They Cost

- No additional funding is needed but there are additional costs for classroom resources and textbooks.

Things to Consider

- Scheduling for a multigrade team can be difficult, especially in extra-curricular or exploratory courses such as band, art, and music. In addition, joining the three grades for physical education can pose problems, so care should be taken with respect to planning physical education activities.

- Care should be taken with respect to the assignment of teachers to content areas. Make sure that teachers are comfortable with their assigned content areas as well as their shared classes. For example, on the Piranha team, all teachers taught mathematics as well as at least one other content area, as well as Critical Thinking and additional courses for individual groups of students. (For additional suggestions, see below.)

Current Progress and Results

- In both schools, teachers, parents, and students report a strong feeling of community and shared responsibility; end-of-year surveys indicate that students had nearly no negative feelings regarding teachers, peers, or schoolwork.

- In both schools, teachers report that they are better able to assess a student's progress and abilities and plan instructional strategies, because they know the student for a much longer period of time and are able to follow progress more closely.

- In both schools, the teachers report that the use of thematic, interdisciplinary instruction is crucial to the success of multigrade instruction.

♦ In both schools, the multigrade teams report greatly reduced discipline problems.

♦ In both schools, administrative and principal support was indicated as extremely important to the success of the approach.

♦ In both schools, student scores on standardized tests are at or above that of the remaining student population.

♦ In both schools, attendance rates for students were similar to the remaining school population's attendance.

Additional Considerations and Implications

Because of the complex nature of this approach the following ideas and considerations for principals, teachers, students, and parents are included.

♦ Implications for the Principal

The following points should be considered when implementing a multigrade/multiyear middle school team:

- Select teachers who are committed to multigrade/multiyear grouping and allow them to be leaders.

- Communicate with the parents prior to the implementation. The parents and the students need to be sold on the concept.

- In the first year of implementation, plan for the fact that eighth grade students may not be happy about being mixed with younger students.

- The teachers need the freedom to organize the team to meet the needs of mixed age classes.

- Be aware that a multigrade/multiyear team will affect the rest of the school in terms of exploratory classes and how data such as attendance or achievement test scores are collected and reported.

- An innovative practice such as multigrade/multiyear teaming will need strong advocates in the form of teachers, parents, students, and administrators.

- Provide the time needed for planning and evaluation for the teachers.

- Plan for the fact that the state or other agencies will want data reported by grade level.
- When necessary, alter school practices that are divided by grade level. Remember when implementing a multigrade team that the school is no longer totally divided according to grade level.
- Plan for scheduling problems such as if band is only taught one period, do the students on the multigrade team get to be in band or not?
- Provide opportunities for students to mix with age mates in all school activities.

♦ Implications for Teachers

- Break the conventional mold of education. Multigrade middle school teams are an innovative practice; don't do the same old thing.
- Realize that you should have different expectations for different students.
- The curriculum needs some individualization.
- Realize that it takes a great deal of time to develop and implement an innovative program.
- No matter how much time it takes, thematic units are an effective way to deliver multigrade instruction.
- Realize that students, parents, and other teachers on your campus may not agree with the concept of multigrade grouping. You will have to become an advocate for multigrade grouping.

♦ Implications for Students

- Realize that you may be isolated from many of your age mates.
- Be aware that you will remain with the same teachers and peers for three years.
- You may have more responsibility for mentoring younger students.
- If you are on a pilot multigrade team, you may feel you are being treated differently.
- You may or may not like being mixed with younger and older students.

- You may have to remain with a teacher you do not like for three years.

- Realize that you may be only one of a few students from your grade level in exploratory classes.

- Older students on the team will be able to help you adjust to a new team. Older students can help you with your assignments or help you open your locker.

- You will have friends of all ages and get to be with the same friends for three years.

♦ Implications for Parents

- Stay involved in your child's education. No matter how much your child may like a multigrade team, it is still your responsibility to stay involved in your child's educational process.

- Find out how multigrade teaming will be implemented at your child's school. Find out how the teachers and principal define multigrade teaming.

- Multigrade teaming is one alternative to traditional grade level grouping. Realize that multigrade teaming is not the answer to all the problems in education. Identify goals of the program at your child's school.

- Multigrade teaming is not for all students.

- Much cooperative learning and group work will be done in a multigrade team. Realize that cooperative learning is an effective instructional strategy.

- Realize that just because you are used to single grade groupings that does not mean single grade groupings are the best educational practice.

- Often, the exploratory classes offered at middle schools are limited. Mixing three grade-levels in one team sometimes limits the exploratory classes even more. All students on a multigrade team have to go to exploratory classes at the same time but the offerings at that time may be limited. For example, at the time your child goes to exploratory only sixth grade band may be offered. That might be a problem for a seventh or eighth grade student that has already had a year or two of band. Work with your child's school to solve such problems.

Contact

Although fictional names, Smith Middle School and Bead Middle School are based on real schools. For more information, contact:

Margaret Heeney
One University Plaza, MSC 5550
Cape Girardeau, MO 63701
Voice: 573-651-2207
Fax: 573-651-2410

Reaching for the Stars

Ormond Stone Middle School, Centreville, Virginia

Interdisciplinary teaming is often called the cornerstone of middle-level education. This team's approach is innovative in that the team has successfully developed a strong team philosophy and structure that could be used as a model for all others.

The Program's Goals

- ◆ Ensure that all students reach their academic and personal potential.

How the Program Works

- ◆ The Shooting Stars team consists of 4 core academic teachers, 1 special education resource teacher, and 140 students of varying abilities.
- ◆ All decisions related to students, curriculum, schedule, or other school matters are team decisions.
- ◆ The team is exceptionally well organized, especially with respect to keeping records and organizing the various forms of information related to the team's activities and goals. For example:
  - Student progress reports are collaboratively completed, with space for comments included for all teachers;
  - Each team meeting has a written agenda and minutes are taken of each meeting;
  - Special meetings, such as parent conferences, student conferences, and administrator interactions are noted;
  - Prereport card student progress sheets are collaboratively completed by the team;
  - The discipline plan and rules are collaboratively developed and infractions noted daily;

- Parent communications, including letters, notes, and newsletters, are noted and discussed each time a communication takes place;

- Records of actions taken, commitments and plans made, are noted and fully explained to parents, teachers, and students.

How the Program is Funded and How Much It Costs

- Interdisciplinary teaming can be slightly more expensive to fund, because of inconsistent student populations. In most cases, however, no additional funding is needed.

Things to Consider

- Flexibility and willingness to cooperate and engage in team activities are important qualifications for team teachers.

- A shared philosophy of education is often necessary.

- Adherence to a shared role definition is often critical; that is, teams need to hold assigned roles and responsibilities for the team to function effectively.

- Communications are extremely important; there should be a steady stream of communication to and from all levels of the team, including parents.

Current Progress and Results

- This team's efforts have been recognized as exemplary throughout the school and school district.

- The team experiences fewer discipline problems and referrals.

- Teachers report that students who once "slipped through the cracks" are being included on the team and much more attention is now given to these students.

- Special education procedures and communications are clearer and better understood by teachers.

- Records and information kept by the team are important sources of discussion with parents and others.

School and Demographic Information

Ormond Stone Middle School
5500 Sully Park Drive
Centreville, VA 20120

- 200+ students, grades 7–8; 20 teachers; diverse population consisting of students living in subsidized housing through upper class; large suburban.

Contact

Natalie Ward
5500 Sully Park Drive
Centreville, VA, 20120
Voice: 703-631-5500

Who Needs a Principal?
The Team Can Do It All!

Angola Middle School,
Angola, Indiana

This innovative team is empowered to manage academics, control and organize for positive student behavior, develop and spend budget monies, communicate among themselves and throughout the school community, coordinate student schedules, and hire new teachers. In addition, this award-winning rural-school team enables students to manage an exceptional service learning project.

The Program's Goals

♦ Demonstrate how empowered teams of teachers can act autonomously and bring about positive school changes, including higher test scores.

♦ Focus on academics as well as behavior and student organization.

How the Program Works

♦ Each teacher on the four-person team teaches a core academic subject as well as language and spelling each day.

♦ Each day begins and ends with a homeroom advisory period.

♦ In order to focus on academics, the team uses:

• Flexible block scheduling;

• Blocked core classes;

• Curriculum and subject integration and thematic instructional approaches;

• Outdoor laboratories and education;

• Numerous field trips;

• Numerous guest speakers from the community;

• Extensive project learning.

♦ With respect to managing student behavior, empowering students, and enhancing self-esteem and motivation, the team uses:

- A strong emphasis on "the positive;"
- Positive postcards mailed to students and parents;
- Social workers and counselors for advisory input and advice;
- Active, hands-on academic and effective approaches to advisory and homeroom;
- Lunchtime team activities;
- Enrichment and remediation courses, help sessions, study halls, and homework assistance;
- A monthly team newsletter to all students' homes;
- A monthly calendar of events;
- A strong orientation program for entering fifth graders from feeder elementary schools;
- An annual overnight "lock-in" for all students and faculty;
- Common procedures, rules, discipline consequences, and steps.

How the Program is Funded and How Much It Costs

♦ The team receives an annual budget of $1,000 to use as the team sees fit.

Things to Consider

♦ It is imperative that teachers have both a common team planning time as well as an individual planning time.

♦ Proper scheduling of students into exploratory, prevocational, and related arts classes is crucial to appropriate planning times.

♦ The flexible block schedule is important to allow for the variations in curriculum and instruction that are often necessary for thematic, interdisciplinary activities.

♦ A focus on academic success is critical for teams to be able to enjoy the empowerment.

Current Progress and Results

◆ Attendance is significantly improved compared to earlier years.

◆ Standardized test scores have risen.

◆ Student and teacher morale is high; students want to be at school.

◆ There is a dramatic decrease in inappropriate student behavior and discipline problems.

◆ Common rules and procedures are appreciated by both students and parents.

◆ The success of this team is being leveraged across the remaining part of the school and school district.

◆ The team has been featured in *The Middle School Journal*.

School and Demographic Information

Angola Middle School
575 E. U.S. Highway 20
Angola, IN 46703

◆ 650+ students, grades 6–8; 42 teachers; 25% free/reduced lunch; 99% white; rural.

Contact

Ann Rice
575 E. U.S. Highway 20
Angola, IN 46703
Voice: 219-665-9581
Fax: 219-665-9583
E-mail: arice@msdsteuben.k12.in.us

It's Our School!

Taylor Middle School, Millbrae, California

This nationally recognized school's approach is particularly innovative in its holistic approach to education. That is, the entire diverse school community takes part in multiple facets of its management, organization, instruction, and climate. Faculty and others from Taylor have presented this school's approach throughout the country and it often has visitors from the United States as well as other nations.

The Program's Goals

♦ Include as wide a range as possible in decision-making and governance at the school and school-community levels.

♦ Create a community of school leaders consisting of students, faculty, and parents.

How the Program Works

♦ The principal and faculty strive to include all elements of the school community in the governance of the school, including goal-setting and assessment.

♦ Faculty members have responsibility and authority for making decisions regarding important educational and instructional elements such as:

  • Interviewing and hiring new personnel;

  • Developing and arranging staff development and teacher-education activities, writing and developing curriculum, selecting textbooks and other educational materials, and deciding on major budget expenditures;

  • Working with university teacher educators as mentors, supervisors, and cooperating teachers for student teachers and practicum students;

  • Writing grants to various funding agencies.

♦ In addition, faculty members often make regional and national presentations about the school and its successes. In addition, they work closely with both parent and student governance and advisory groups.

♦ Parents are very active in the school, where their participation is welcomed and valued. The 40-member board of the Parent-Teacher Association works closely with school community members as volunteers, managing a student store, as translators (there are 36 different languages spoken in the school), raising funds for the school, supervising field trips, developing and writing newsletters, managing a homework center, managing a Spanish homework center, and working with teachers. Also, parents representing each grade level work with student council members for goal setting and communications.

♦ Students at Taylor actively work to enhance the school's climate and goals as peer helpers, conflict resolution managers, and peer tutors. Students also host other school community meetings, and often attend School Board and City Council meetings.

How the Program is Funded and How Much It Costs

♦ Little extra cost is incurred for these programs; rather, extensive time and effort are made toward maintaining the school's commitment to excellence.

Things to Consider

♦ The successes that Taylor consistently experiences are not those that can be expected to happen quickly. All individuals involved must realize that a great deal of time and energy is necessary to reach this level of total school commitment.

♦ Relationships are critical to a holistic approach, and as most human endeavors, relationships take time to grow, evolve, and mature. Care should be taken to guide the formation of strong relationships without forcing people into uncomfortable positions.

♦ Trust is also critical and cannot be developed quickly, nor without a strong commitment to relationship building across the community.

Current Progress and Results

♦ Students consistently do extremely well in academic achievement comparisons.

♦ Due to the substantive investment made by people within the school community toward the school's goals, celebration of success is an important part of the school's culture. The school has been awarded the California Distinguished School and Blue Ribbon Awards, and care is taken to recognize all community members for their contributions.

♦ Because of the school's unique location adjacent to San Francisco International Airport, it also receives frequent visitors from around the world.

♦ The school has also been cited in a number of books and articles regarding exemplary middle school practices.

School and Demographic Information

Taylor Middle School
850 Taylor Blvd.
Millbrae, CA 94030

♦ 800+ students, grades 6–8; 50% white, 50% minority (36 different native languages) school population largely representative of larger city population (equal proportions of low-, middle-, and upper-income families); large suburban.

Contact

Sharon Fritz
850 Taylor Blvd.
Millbrae, CA 94030
Voice: 415-697-4096
Fax: 415-697-8435

2

Instruction, Curriculum, and Assessment

This chapter presents a variety of ideas and programs that surround the core of what we do in middle schools: We teach, we develop and respond to curriculum, and we assess how well students have mastered what we have tried to teach. In many states, the curriculum is developed and mandated by legislative actions, and in others, more responsibility for curriculum development is in the hands of teachers and local educators and communities. Throughout the country there are associations and institutions that attempt to define curriculum for teachers and schools in their respective fields. There are few, if any, teachers who are not responding to recent standards in mathematics that have been put forth by the National Council of Teachers of Mathematics. But regardless of where the curriculum comes from, it remains the "what" of our efforts, in conjunction with creating learning environments that are conducive to the early adolescent's development.

Concurrent with the development of curricula, there is a great deal of attention being paid to the "how" of what teachers do. Instructional methods have become conversational topics for politicians, teachers, administrators, parents, and others who are interested in the education of our nation's children. However the interest arises, it is still the teachers who carry out these instructional techniques each day; it is teachers who create, test, adopt, adapt, change, and use the techniques to make learning meaningful and relevant.

Finally, teachers assess and evaluate. Teachers do this for many reasons, but the two primary reasons for assessment and evaluation are to determine how well a topic or a subject was taught, and to see how well students understand the concept or how well they can perform the skill we taught. Teachers have long known that simple paper and pencil classroom tests as well as nationally normed, standardized tests tell us relatively little with respect to what we have actually taught each day in the classroom. We are constantly looking for more and better ways to assess, and we are constantly seeking ways to combine our instructional methods with assessments in order to more effectively assess learning. As long as schools are subject to political or governmental examination and accountability, we will also be forced to administer tests that measure how well our students have mastered the curriculum. And this is the way it should be, for as professionals we must constantly seek methods for improvement and methods to remain accountable for our actions.

This chapter is divided into three parts. The first part, curriculum, has innovative, creative, and unique programs that integrate different concepts and content, that challenge us to continually work at grouping students in ways that help students learn, and that help us examine and use a curriculum that is meaningful and relevant to our students.

The second part has exceptionally effective and innovative instructional methods and approaches that combine technology, skill development, meaningful student assignments, and rigor. The final part consists of unique approaches to assessments, including ways to more authentically measure learning and skills development.

Curriculum

These programs are excellent examples of innovative and creative approaches to curriculum:

Kids to Kids International: Rochambeau Middle (Connecticut)

> Middle school uses an international book program that links language arts, English, and social studies in cross-cultural studies

"Changes"—Invention and Transportation: Willis Middle (Ohio)

> Real-life, thematic unit that makes meaningful connections between school and the world of work using industrial partnerships

Foundational Approaches in Science Teaching: FAST (Hawaii)

> Award-winning science program based on thinking and process skills, foundational concepts, hands-on, and discovery learning

Watershed: A Whole-Learning Experience: Radnor Middle (Pennsylvania)

> Uses the Watershed integrated program to replace most of the grade-level curriculum with multiple teaching methods and hands-on, active approaches

Explorations in Language and Art: Black River Middle (New Jersey)

> Writing program that links student interests, creativity, motivation, and performances into an effective integrated whole

Brought to You By… A Look at Advertising in the Middle: William English Middle (Indiana)

> Integrated approach to language arts and the fine arts that is strongly linked to the world of work, community service, and applied learning

Revisiting the 20s and 30s: Hines Middle (Virginia)

> A large school's creative approach to using the fine arts as the central point around which academic content and state standards are joined and linked together

Changing from Shop to Career Education and Technology: Clark-Pleasant Middle (Indiana)

Former school curriculum for shop restructured and rewritten to include 15 high-tech instructional modules linked to academic subjects

Kids to Kids International

Rochambeau Middle School, Southbury, Connecticut

This international picture book program is extremely innovative in the manner in which the program links social studies, international understanding, language arts and writing, and cross-grade communication. In addition, the success of the program in this middle school is spreading into the elementary grades, as students from the middle school teach the project to third grade children in another school.

The Program's Goals

- ◆ To provide an opportunity for middle school students to learn about children in other countries and cultures.

- ◆ To provide an integrated writing approach to students that has meaning and connections with other subjects.

- ◆ To provide an opportunity for students and teachers to communicate across grade levels and schools.

How the Program Works

- ◆ Students write and create picture books about themselves and other aspects of American life and send them to children in other countries. Students choose a country or geographic area and complete an investigation of the country and its cultures.

- ◆ Variations to the process include, but are not limited to, groups of students preparing a single book, students creating individual books, cross-age groups of students creating books, older students teaching the writing process to younger students, and pairs of students working on a book.

- ◆ Students often use a concept-web approach to develop their respective books, and follow a carefully taught writing-process approach that ensures carefully developed topics, well-written books, and carefully crafted pieces.

- Students carefully create pictures and illustrations to support and enhance their writing. Attention is paid to proper binding of the books and many pages are laminated. An author's page is also included with pictures of the authors, brief biographical information, contact information, and so forth.

- Completed books are shipped to Kids to Kids International, a nonprofit organization that forwards the books to the appropriate countries.

- Artistic supplies (markers, crayons, paper, etc.) are also shipped with the books to encourage children in the receiving culture to make and send a book back to the students.

How the Program is Funded and How Much It Costs

- Costs are minimal and well within the reach of most schools' budgets. Most of the costs are for purchase of artistic materials to include with the books that are sent to other countries. Shipping costs are minimal, because the books are shipped to New York rather than to the foreign country.

- A teacher's manual ($5.00) is available from Kids to Kids International, 1961 Commerce Street, Yorktown Heights, NY 10598.

- Parent-Teacher Organizations as well as student fund-raising can be used to provide funds needed for the project. Supplies can also be donated by local businesses.

Things to Consider

- American children often have inaccurate views of other countries, so take care that the children have a factual and nonstereotypical understanding of the cultures and countries to which their books will be sent.

- Students should be careful to write and illustrate books using appropriate themes. For example, it is inappropriate to send materials depicting violence to a country experiencing civil war or unrest. It is very important for teachers to monitor the books' content and illustrations throughout the process.

Current Progress and Results

♦ The program has been in effect for over six years, and hundreds of books have been shipped to children in countries such as Cambodia, Russia, Lithuania, and South Africa.

♦ Because of the success of the program, it has spread to other schools in the area.

♦ Students in the school indicate a new understanding of other cultures and demonstrate a higher degree of tolerance for differences.

School and Demographic Information

Rochambeau Middle School
100 Peter Road
Southbury, CT 06488

♦ 650+ students, grades 5–8; 75 teachers and staff; 95% white; middle class; suburban

Contact

Monica Leavitt
70 Marvelwood Drive
New Haven, CT 06515
Voice: 203-387-6713
E-mail: mlmentor@connix.com

"Changes"—Invention and Transportation

Willis Middle School, Delaware, Ohio

This middle school's interdisciplinary approach is truly innovative in the way the school and the unit make real-life connections with the world of work. Students work on various design and engineering problems with people from one of the school's industrial partners.

The Program's Goals

- ◆ To allow students to see the connections between academic work and the industrial and engineering worlds.

- ◆ To allow students to collect and manage data from a variety of sources toward the development and design of new safety features for buses.

- ◆ To allow students to see how their work can be utilized and incorporated into new industrial designs.

How the Program Works

- ◆ A comprehensive interdisciplinary teaching unit is used to incorporate as many subjects as possible into a thematic unit based on the concept of safety. This central concept is linked to the school's industrial partner, a local builder of buses; students then invent, develop, and design features to improve the safety of the buses.

- ◆ Throughout the unit, visits by individuals from the local bus company are woven through the student's activities. Students also take field trips to a design and engineering firm to look at how designs are developed and to the manufacturing plant to view and experience how the assembly line process operates.

- ◆ Buses of various types are brought to the school for students to examine and compare.

- ◆ Guest speakers, ranging from individuals from design firms to bus drivers, are incorporated throughout the unit and scheduled in such a way that the speakers give their presentations during the time frame that students are working on the part of their designs that the speaker's presentation addresses.

How the Program is Funded and How Much It Costs

- ◆ The program is funded through the school's partnership with the bus manufacturing company. The company provides released time for its employees to participate, as well as new buses for the students to evaluate. The company also allows 280 students to take an extensive tour of their plant over a six-day period.

- ◆ The major costs for the school are the transportation costs for the students to visit the plant. Individual students pay for their respective costs, and scholarships are provided for those unable to pay for the trip.

Things to Consider

- ◆ Although the focus of this unit is on bus design and safety, the activities and integrated academic portions could be easily adapted to any local industrial or manufacturing business.

- ◆ Careful attention to detail, especially those details involving student movement or guests is important. In this case, careful planning was needed in order to have 280 students visit the manufacturing plant over a six-day period.

- ◆ It is also important for teachers to carefully coordinate and plan the various subject-matter expectations involved in the academic portions of the unit.

Current Progress and Results

- ◆ Student evaluations of the project indicated overwhelming support and enjoyment of the unit.

- ◆ Students indicated that they gained valuable insights into many careers and jobs that they previously didn't know existed.

- Students indicated that they saw how the various aspects of academic work fit within industry and how various subjects are used on a daily basis.

- Students indicated that they felt important and valuable as they became a part of the local business community.

- Individuals from the manufacturing company indicated that they enjoyed and benefitted from their involvement with the school and the students.

- The school received positive notoriety from the community as well as support for its programs.

School and Demographic Information

Willis Middle School
74 W. William Street
Delaware, OH 43015

- 870+ students, grades 6–8; 100 teachers and staff; 93% white; 25% free/reduced lunch; small urban

Contact

Teresa F. Bettae
74 W. William Street
Delaware, OH 43015
Voice: 614-369-8728
Fax: 614-363-6940

Foundational Approaches in Science Teaching (FAST)

University of Hawaii at Manoa, Manoa, Hawaii

This award-winning and nationally recognized program in teaching science is uniquely integrative and appropriate for middle-level students. Based on developing thinking skills, laboratory skills, and knowledge of foundational concepts of science, the program is currently used in 38 states and 10 foreign countries; over 450,000 students per year are exposed to this especially effective approach.

The Program's Goals

- ◆ To develop scientific literacy for all students.

- ◆ To develop thinking skills.

- ◆ To develop laboratory skills.

- ◆ To help students understand and build knowledge about foundational scientific concepts.

How the Program Works

- ◆ Based on the premise that schooling's primary purpose is to develop every student's intellectual capacities, the program focuses on providing intellectually stimulating, rigorous, hands-on activities and curricula directed toward preparing students to participate in transactions in a dynamic society that is founded on science and technology. FAST students engage in a carefully sequenced set of experiential, hands-on learning activities that are connected to students' previous experiences and knowledge.

- ◆ Students work in investigative research teams that plan and execute investigations, discuss and validate hypotheses, and summarize and draw conclusions. Rather than disseminating knowledge, the teacher facilitates group instruction, and maintains the investigative environment, sets up tasks, gives suggestions, and helps students evaluate their experiences.

♦ The subject matter is organized into three strands: physical science, ecology, and relational study. The first two strands provide the formal science content, and the third strand integrates science, technology, and society. Skills and knowledge are often used to cross content from one scientific field to another. The relational study strand is also used to demonstrate the social implications of science and technology and how the various elements of the content and processes can be used to help human beings make good decisions regarding the societal aspects of science and technology.

♦ 70% to 80% of students' time is spent either in laboratory settings or in field studies; 20% to 30% of the time they are involved in analyzing data, working in small groups, examining other literature related to the ideas, and writing.

♦ Students manage their learning and investigations using several organizers:

- A student book with background information, guides to research, and summary questions;

- A record/log book in which notes, diagrams, observations, and other records of student work;

- A set of reference books that help students become proficient users of the various instruments and materials used in their investigations, and that provide supplemental information.

♦ Teachers are trained to use this comprehensive method of instruction through a teacher institute that provides information and strategies regarding laboratory and field exercises that are to be carried out through the year; instruction on using inquiry methods and strategies; instruction and information on organizing and managing the classroom; and ways to address student deficiencies, mathematics, and evaluation. The training is critical to proper use and implementation of FAST. Several follow-up sessions are also provided, especially during the first year of implementation through which teachers share experiences and offer ideas.

How the Program is Funded and How Much It Costs

♦ The ten-day FAST teacher institute costs $500 per participant and includes a set of teacher materials. Classroom instructional materials average about $1,000; yearly replacement costs average about $100 to $200 depending on the number of students.

Things to Consider

♦ This program is very flexible and can accommodate a variety of school schedules including various types of block schedules. Developed by the Curriculum Research and Development Group at the University of Hawaii, it has been in use for a number of years.

♦ Careful, comprehensive planning for staff development is crucial to the success of the program. In addition, the program will work best if the decision to use FAST is collaboratively made and includes teachers from disciplines other than science and technology.

♦ Adopters of the program should also consider comprehensive follow-up training and support. As in many staff development activities, the more comprehensive the follow-up support, the more likely the adoption will have the desired results.

♦ The program's flexibility allows its use in meeting a variety of state-mandated objectives or curricula.

Current Progress and Results

♦ The program has been validated, recognized, and named as exemplary by such organizations as the National Science Teachers Association, the National Diffusion Network, the United States Department of Education, and many leading scientists.

♦ The program addresses science standards developed by the American Association for the Advancement of Science (AAAS) as well as the standards developed by the National Center for Improving Science Education.

♦ Several comprehensive evaluative studies have been undertaken to compare student achievement of students using the FAST approach with students who have not been exposed to the FAST approach. In nearly every field (content, laboratory skills, and thinking skills), FAST students consistently perform to statistically significant higher levels of achievement. In addition, significant differences have been found between FAST and non-FAST students regarding achievement in high school biology; greater interest in further study of science; students choosing science as a hobby; students demonstrating greater inquiry-oriented cognitive preferences; and students showing high preference for critical questioning as a mode of learning.

School and Demographic Information

University Laboratory School
Curriculum Research and Development Group
University of Hawaii
1776 University Avenue
Honolulu, HI 96822

◆ 350 students, grades K-12; 75 teachers/staff; very diverse population; urban

Contact

Donald B. Young
Coordinator of Science Education Research
1775 University Avenue
Honolulu, HI 96822
Voice: 808-956-7863
Fax: 808-956-9486
E-mail: crdg@hawaii.edu

Watershed: A Whole-Learning Program

Radnor Middle School, Wayne, Pennsylvania

This innovative seventh grade integrated program is unique in several ways:

- It replaces the entire traditional, subject-centered curriculum for the entire school year;

- The curriculum is entirely based on the concept of a watershed and learning as a process;

- Parents and student apply for admission into the program and are assigned to the program based on a random selection;

- No grades are used in the program as student progress is monitored and communicated through other methods;

- The program is actually less expensive than traditional approaches;

- Students are immersed in the program for nearly the full day every day, with the exception of a short period that is set aside for writing instruction;

- Students do as well as or better than other students on standardized tests.

Due to the complex and comprehensive nature of this program, its description is more lengthy than others in this book.

The Program's Goals

- To create a learning environment in which students accept responsibility for learning.

- To provide students with an awareness of the relevance of learning and of their personal connections with materials covered and to demonstrate the interrelatedness of all learning.

- To emphasize the importance of fundamental thinking and communication skills, and to encourage learning from primary rather than secondary sources.

- To create a learning environment which promotes cooperative learning instead of competitive learning.

- To illustrate that education is best achieved when it is a cooperative venture shared by teachers, students, and parents; and, to that end, to maximize the parental involvement in the learning process.

- To demonstrate that leaning is a life-long pursuit, which transcends the limits of the school's walls.

- To emphasize the ecological, historical, economic, political, and cultural importance of watersheds.

How the Program Works

- The program's emphasis is on processes. Using the senses of place, time, and quality as organizing elements, students engage in extensive examination and work that focuses on a watershed.

- With respect to a sense of place, students are required to participate in various activities and produce a number of learning products including, but not limited to:

  - Creating accurate maps and drawings of the watershed region including important landmarks;

  - Creating scaled, three-dimensional topological maps of the region;

  - Conducting extensive field studies using physical, chemical, and biological parameters, and charting the results and their interpretations;

  - Demonstrating an understanding of photosynthesis and respiration and their connections to systemic energy flows, such as those in the human body, food chains, and regional development;

  - Demonstrating knowledge about water—its physical characteristics and its influences on all aspects of life;

  - Describing the characteristics of a stream and their connections to topography and ecosystems;

- Identifying organisms found in and around local streams and drawing conclusions about their forms, structures, and ecological functions;

- Recognizing and describing major regional rock types by characteristics, age, location, topological significance, and historical influence;

- Writing a "drip essay" that follows the path of a drop of water along a stream and through the water cycle.

♦ With respect to a sense of time, students are required to participate in a variety of activities and produce a number of learning products including, but not limited to:

- Creating an "American Diary" with certain events chronologically listed in a manner that shows student understanding of a particular group of people who lived in the region at different times;

- Participating in the planning and presentation of group projects based on historical events and groups;

- Researching a specified portion of the nineteenth century and creating a newspaper that displays the results of the research;

- Planning, conducting, and presenting an oral history covering an aspect of twentieth-century life.

♦ With respect to a sense of quality, students are required to participate in a variety of activities and produce a number of learning products including, but not limited to:

- Researching and creating a facsimile of a painting by one of the Wyeths;

- Creating a human body map that shows the major organs and systems and leading a tour of at least one system;

- Creating a story that describes a fantastic voyage through the human body detailing the location and function of various organs and systems;

- Designing a home, which design includes scaled floor plans, plot diagrams, elevations, and scale models;

- Producing and presenting a regional plan for the area for the year 2020 which demonstrates an understanding of regional systems.

♦ At appropriate times throughout the year, students also conduct field tests on water quality, take field trips, and write about their learning and experiences.

How the Program is Funded and How Much It Costs

♦ The program actually costs less than the traditional model. All funds come from the local school district and are budgeted in a manner similar to that of a separate grade level or department.

♦ The annual operating budget costs are approximately $170.00 per student, which includes all classroom supplies, materials, and field trip expenses, as well as the various computer and technology supplies needed to run the program.

Things to Consider

♦ This is a very nontraditional approach to learning and runs counter to many approaches to middle-level education. It is, therefore, important that those interested in developing a similar program hold similar educational philosophies and visions.

♦ Such a program is not easily implemented without a great deal of extensive planning and attention to detail.

♦ Some resistance to such a program is natural. The program can be very convincing based on its success and the extent to which students perform and improve skills, self-esteem, and attitudes.

Current Progress and Results

♦ In its eleventh year, the program has been extremely successful in a number of ways. It has provided hundreds of students an opportunity to link learning and schooling to relevant, meaningful activities and tasks, as well as helping students master basic skills.

♦ Students in the program do as well as or better than peers on standardized tests, and develop better reading and writing skills at a faster pace than their peers.

♦ Students show greater independence in learning and have more positive attitudes about learning and school. Students also show greater skill at mastering their time and take greater responsibility for their own learning.

♦ Anecdotal information from parents and students attest to the program's many successes.

School and Demographic Information

Radnor Middle School
131 South Wayne Avenue
Wayne, PA 19087

♦ 1,000+ students, grades 5–8; 80 teachers; 80% white; middle/upper-class; suburban

Contact

Mark Springer or Ed Silcox
131 South Wayne Avenue
Wayne, PA 19087
Voice: 610-688-8100 ext. 271
Fax: 610-688-2491
E-mail: mspringe@itrc.dciu.k12.pa.us

Explorations in Language and Art

Black River Middle School, Chester, New Jersey

This unique approach to teaching and improving students' writing skills is based on incorporating a number of effective strategies that not only improve writing, but improve students' motivation, creativity, understanding of the fine arts, and performance. Students produce original works in the fields of writing, drawing, painting, and sculpting.

The Program's Goals

♦ To use the complementary areas of language arts and fine arts to enhance and improve students' written and oral expression, critical thinking skills, and reading.

♦ To create a learning environment that encourages the incorporation of multiple intelligences by students as well as teachers.

How the Program Works

♦ Heterogeneously grouped students meet every day in a traditional 40- to 50-minute period. Students with special needs are included as feasible and appropriate. A standard classroom is equipped with a video camera, TV, VCR, a 35mm camera, and one or more computers.

♦ Using a teacher-student team approach, students work to create original art and other works that incorporate writing and editing as central to the work. Students produce videos, films, photographs, drawings, paintings, and sculpture as they capture an idea or concept. Writing exercises as well as editing and peer reviews take place throughout the initial stages of creating the art as students describe their work and how it relates to other areas of the fine arts.

♦ The concepts of composition, form, style, shape, and function are interwoven into the writing as well as into the student's creative works; students are given the opportunity to make the connections among these concepts and other real-life applications. For example, toward the end of the year, each student studies contemporary and historical advertising and marketing, including demographic analyses, form and structure, media placement, and production. Students create a product and develop an advertising campaign for their original products; advertising professionals from the community assist with the students' work as visiting teachers and guest speakers.

♦ A wide variety of strategies are incorporated in the teaching environment including:

- Role playing and simulations;

- Motivational exercises and activities;

- Prewriting and discussions;

- Real-world applications of artistic and written works;

- Local writers and artists as guest speakers and teachers;

- Local video-production experts as guest speakers and teachers.

♦ Other teachers in the building with expertise in the fine arts or other crafts or technologies assist with various student works.

How the Program is Funded and How Much It Costs

♦ The annual budget for this program is about $1,000 for textbooks, supplies, binders, video-production supplies, publication costs, and art supplies. The local cable-TV company provides access to cable in the classroom at no cost.

Things to Consider

♦ Teachers using this approach should have a working knowledge of multiple intelligences and learning styles in order to be able to create and use a variety of effective strategies. Students should also be taught how these intelligences function in every individual.

♦ Teachers considering this approach should be team players and be able to work with other faculty members who have expertise in other areas, particularly the fine arts.

- Parents and others from the community should be encouraged to visit and participate in the classes, especially if they bring a particular talent or skill to share with the students.

- Administrative support and commitment are needed.

Current Progress and Results

- Each year students publish their best works in video or book form and the works are shared with the larger school community.

- Students' achievement in English and language arts has improved.

- Students view the learning of English and writing as fundamental and necessary as well as fun.

- Community awareness of the school and the students' work has increased significantly.

- Local businesses and other professionals have become more aware of the school, its program, and its successes; attitudes toward the middle school have improved.

- Various aspects of the program have been featured at local, regional, and national conferences, as well as on local television stations.

School and Demographic Information

Black River Middle School
Route #513
Chester, NJ 07930

- 350 students, grades 6–8; 34 teachers; 99% white; middle class; suburban

Contact

Joseph S. Pizzo
237 West High Street
Bound Brook, NJ 08805
Voice: 908-879-6363
Fax: 908-879-9085

Brought to You By... A Look at Advertising in the Middle

William H. English Middle School, Scottsburg, Indiana

This creative and innovative integrated language arts and fine arts program is unique in its depth and breadth and how it links to charitable institutions in the community. It also provides for student mastery of a variety of skills and competencies that rely on higher order thinking, creativity, and an understanding of the economic realities of contemporary culture.

The Program's Goals

- To familiarize students with the field of advertising and related economic theory.

- To help student make more effective consumer choices.

- To improve reading, writing, speaking, and communications skills.

- To help students make connections with social and charitable groups outside of the school and instill a sense of caring for fellow human beings.

- To help students strengthen cooperative skills and the ability to work in groups.

How the Program Works

- In this six-week unit of study, language arts and fine arts are combined and integrated into a set of learning activities. Students are grouped in a variety of ways in order to make the best use of combing the two subjects.

- Small groups of advertising "companies" are formed. The students manage their respective companies by choosing logos, themes, mottos, and names, and by preparing to produce a marketable product. Each "company" receives a set amount of play money with which to start their business. To expose students to how real markets and economies function, several activities are designed to simulate the business world.

♦ In art classes, each student company designs and produces a marketable product to be sold to make money that will be donated to a local charity at the end of the unit.

♦ In language arts classes, students study advertising language, persuasive speech, word usage, grammar, and proper writing. In addition, they investigate a number of charities by writing business letters to the groups asking for information.

♦ Video and audio ads and other art works are produced to support their respective products.

♦ Students hold a "Market Day" during which the student companies sell their products and make business decisions about marketing and pricing. The money raised from this event is donated to a local charity.

♦ Each student group develops and maintains a portfolio of all work related to the project, which portfolio contains items and assignments related to the project and their products.

♦ An extensive grading and scoring guide, or rubric, is used to evaluate each aspect of the students' work that is included in the portfolio. Rubrics are used for both the language arts class and the art class.

How the Program is Funded and How Much It Costs

♦ The program costs little beyond normal classroom supplies and art materials. Student "companies" invest minimal amounts of money to produce their respective products for sale.

Things to Consider

♦ To prepare for this unit or a similar one, scheduling the activities well in advance is beneficial.

♦ Supervision of various groups can be a problem if not scheduled and managed well.

Current Progress and Results

♦ Students and teachers indicated that the students improved thinking skills and decision-making skills during the program.

♦ Parents and others outside of the school community responded to the program in very positive ways, which enhanced the school's stature in the community.

♦ Student writing and speaking skills improved.

♦ Cooperation and behavior in group work were significantly better than in previous activities.

♦ A local charitable organization received a donation.

School and Demographic Information

William H. English Middle School
145 South Third St.
Scottsburg, IN 47170

♦ 680 students, grades 6–8; 36 teachers; 99% white; low socioeconomic conditions; rural

Contact

Kathy Anderkin or Karen Chilman
William H. English Middle School
145 South Third St.
Scottsburg, IN 47170
Voice: 812-752-3580

Revisiting the 20s and 30s: History Through the Arts

Hines Middle School, Newport News, Virginia

It is rare to find the arts acting as the framework around which subject-matter content is taught—which is just what Hines Middle School does each year for several weeks. This unique schoolwide approach helps students go beyond historic facts and events and relate to the music, drama, and literature of a unique American era.

The Program's Goals

♦ To implement an effective, schoolwide interdisciplinary unit.

♦ To create a heightened sense of awareness about a unique period of time in our nation's history by providing external stimuli needed to simulate life experiences during this era.

♦ To demonstrate how music, the arts, technology, life skills, and literature are vital tools for reflecting social, emotional, and physical conditions of an era.

♦ To create a schoolwide atmosphere that promotes learning in a variety of styles.

How the Program Works

♦ The program is managed and coordinated by the school librarian and the school's art teacher. Together they selected this theme, wrote for a small state grant, and coordinated all of the activities related to this very comprehensive project. The grant was awarded from the state's arts commission and paid for materials and other expenses associated with the unit.

♦ Planning began early in the year and included these actions:

  • Meeting with the core curriculum teachers regularly to gather ideas and activity plans to insure content and subject area standards were being met;

- Meeting with other exploratory teachers to arrange for their participation and inclusion in the project;

- Developing and distributing a comprehensive time-line that listed and scheduled all events and planning activities needed;

- Reviewing all of the information that was gathered from each of the teachers and revising and redistributing the schedule;

- Contacting and planning for external speakers, artists, and other community individuals involved in the unit;

- Planning for guest appearances and workshops for students;

- Constructing props and stage arrangements for speakers and events;

- Compiling a final calendar of events and final class schedule for the unit.

♦ During the actual unit implementation, the students participated in these activities and events, as well as others:

- A giant marquee was hung in the entry foyer that announced the week's events and activities;

- Each morning's schoolwide announcements included historical facts about the era;

- Core academic teachers in all grades presented materials and gave a variety of assignments related to this period of history;

- Students created exhibits and displays of historic artifacts, events, and historical information;

- Storytellers from the community told tales about the period;

- Visiting artists presented materials, artifacts, and historical information about the era, and several of them gave after-school workshops in different art media;

- Several guests were featured over the school's closed-circuit television system so that all students could hear the speakers;

- Literary and dramatic readings were performed over the school's public address system;

- Students reenacted historical events for other classes of students;

- A school mural highlighting the works of Stuart Davis and Aaron Douglas, noted artists of the era, was dedicated.

How the Program is Funded and How Much It Costs

- ◆ Funds came from several sources, including the school's operating funds, a grant from the state's arts council, and a local business that is one of the school's community partners.

- ◆ Some of the funds were used to pay small honorariums to some of the artists and speakers, and the remaining funds were used to pay for additional materials and supplies needed for the event.

- ◆ The entire project cost less than $1,000 and other schools may be able to implement a program similar to this one for much less, depending on the extent to which the school implements the project.

Things to Consider

- ◆ Planning is critical for such a schoolwide event or project, and it is important to note that this project was planned and coordinated by two teachers who are not core-curriculum subject teachers. Time for meetings and planning should be provided for anyone who coordinates such a comprehensive project.

- ◆ Serious consideration should be given to meeting state subject-matter or content standards, as well as to how to implement various arts projects.

- ◆ Faculty and administrative support for a schoolwide program is critical to its success.

Current Progress and Results

- ◆ Because the project included all of the students in all grade levels, the program will be implemented in three-year cycles. No data regarding student achievement in the area of meeting state standards are available as yet, but it is expected that all students will perform better due to this event and the depth to which the events of the eras were studied.

School and Demographic Information

H.J. Hines Middle School
561 McLawhorne Drive
Newport News, VA 23601-3818

♦ 1450+ students, grades 6–8; 95 teachers; 45% white, 49% African American, 6% other; 40% free and reduced lunch; large urban

Contact

Carolyn Shird or Norma King
561 McLawhorne Drive
Newport News, VA 23601-3818
Voice: 757-591-4878
Fax: 757-591-0119
E-mail: nking@www.hines.nn.k12.va.us *or*
        cshird@www.hines.nn.k12.va.us
School Web page: www.trojan.hines.nn.k12.va.us/I-Gear/

Changing from Shop to Career Education and Technology

Clark-Pleasant Middle School, Whiteland, Indiana

This middle school's move from a traditional industrial education curriculum to a contemporary, career- and technology-based curriculum involved the development of exciting and useful instructional modules, a change from "teacher as information presenter" to "teacher as facilitator," and integration of the academic core subjects into the program.

The Program's Goals

- ◆ To prepare students for a technologically based twenty-first century.

- ◆ To give students opportunities to explore various technology-based careers.

- ◆ To incorporate the academic subject areas into a technology-based curriculum model.

- ◆ To create a modular instructional delivery system that is relevant, meaningful, hands-on, and self-paced.

How the Program Works

- ◆ The exploratory and vocational arts teachers, with the assistance of the school's core academic teachers, created 15 curriculum modules to replace the existing traditionally designed industrial arts (shop) program.

- ◆ The 15 modules presently in use are:
  - Aerodynamics Technology: students design, create, test, analyze, and modify an airplane wing;
  - Audio Communications: students create, script, edit, and produce a series of radio broadcasts that are aired to all students;

- Computer-Aided Drawing: students use CAD technology to draw, create, and adapt three-dimensional forms and figures to industrial applications;

- Computer Applications: students use digital cameras, optical character recognition systems, scanners, and other computer-based applications to design and create a brochure;

- Computer Graphics and Animation: students use digitized images and other hardware and software to create, change, and enhance images;

- Introduction to Electricity: students work with applications of the principles of electricity and electronics to design and create specific circuits and applications;

- Energy, Power, and Transportation: students work with engines, motors, solar power, and other alternative energy sources;

- Introduction to laser Technology: students work with and use lasers to become familiar with theoretical applications, applied laser uses, and the mathematics of lasers;

- Robotics: students work with and build servomotor actuators, gears, beams, and other robotic mechanisms on a five-axis robot;

- Research and Development: students investigate automotive design and aerodynamic theories, use tools and machines, and work with statistical measurements and graphics;

- Structural Technology: students design, create, and build a bridge that meets a number of construction standards;

- Tools and Machines: students use machine tools to manufacture items to close tolerances;

- Video Productions: students learn to operate cameras, generate computer graphics and special effects, and produce a 15-minute video to be shown around the school;

- Virtual Architecture: students use three-dimensional modeling and visualization to design and create structures;

- Visual Communications: students use various forms of drafting tools and instruments, and work with scaling and dimensional information.

♦ Students opt for various modules with the teachers' assistance.

How the Program is Funded and How Much It Costs

◆ The program costs are absorbed through the normal school operating budget; the cost per student is no greater than in the former program.

Things to Consider

◆ Planning and coordinating with all people involved are critical and should be done thoroughly prior to implementation.

◆ Be prepared for some teacher resistance, as this format is very different from traditional instructional methodology.

Current Progress and Results

◆ The modules have been extremely successful, both in terms of academic achievement and in how students view the course and subjects.

School and Demographic Information

Clark-Pleasant Middle School
222 Tracy Street
Whiteland, IN 46184

◆ 680 students, grades 6–8; 40 teachers; 99% white; middle class; small urban

Contact

Philip Wagoner
222 Tracy Street
Whiteland, IN 46184
Voice: 317-535-7121
Fax: 317-535-2064
E-mail: pwagoner@cpcsc.k12.in.us

Instruction

These programs demonstrate effective and innovative instructional methods and approaches that combine technology, skills development, meaningful student assignments, and rigor:

Motivating for Science in a Magnet School for the Arts: Roosevelt Magnet (Illinois)

> A magnet school for the arts takes a creative and unusual approach to getting students involved in science and related activities

Leveling Up, not Watering Down: The Successful Transition to Heterogenous Grouping: Wayland Middle (Massachusetts)

> School uses creative ways to move students formerly in the "low" groups into challenging, rigorous, and accelerated "high" classes

Buckeye Blockbuster—A Whole-School Interdisciplinary Project: Eastwood Middle (Ohio)

> Academics and social values as well as skills are emphasized in this school's approach to an interdisciplinary thematic unit that is managed and coordinated by exploratory and prevocational teachers

Realistic Reading: Hightower Trail Middle (Georgia)

> Year-long reading program that integrates citizenship, technology, problem-solving, and decision-making into improving reading and writing skills

The National Student Research Center: Mandeville Middle (Louisiana)

> Students participate in electronic school district to solve real-life problems and integrate science content, skills, and literacy across the curriculum

TEAMS: Technology Enhancing Achievement in Middle School: Institute for School Innovation (Florida)

> Four Florida middle schools use this program, which integrates technology, learning stations, and interdisciplinary instruction across four disciplines

Motivating for Science in a Magnet School for the Arts

Roosevelt Magnet School, Peoria, Illinois

Motivating students to engage in meaningful science activities in the middle school grades is doubly difficult when the school is a magnet school for students interested in the arts. This unique science education program uses two innovative methods for motivating students: relevance and depth of understanding. It is also unusual in that seventh and eighth grade students often work with younger students in the lower grades as part of their assessments.

The Program's Goals

- ◆ To enrich the existing science curriculum.

- ◆ To provide motivation, excitement, and enthusiasm for science in a school designed to encourage the arts.

- ◆ To increase student awareness of the relevance of science in students' lives.

- ◆ To use a variety of media to instruct as well as to motivate students' interest in science.

How the Program Works

- ◆ Through extensive planning and effective pacing of instruction, the science education program for seventh and eighth grade students takes place during the regular school schedule, which consists of eight 43-minute periods per day.

- ◆ During the regular science periods, the traditional and adopted curriculum is enhanced by improving existing instructional activities by creative approaches to the curriculum. For example, eighth grade students take part in a unit that includes frog dissection, during which students view a videotape about dissection, hear toad and frog calls played, eat frog-shaped candies, and are awarded glow-in-the-dark frogs as prizes. Students are given "Dr. of Frogology" cards on completion of the unit. In addition, the students demonstrate their knowledge, skills, and understanding of anatomy by presenting information and demonstrations to primary grade students.

♦ Other innovative approaches to the traditional curriculum include building primate skeleton models in conjunction with and with the help of primary grade students, snacking on baked insects after a unit about insects, linking National Football League injury reports to an anatomy unit, and making use of other creative links to students' lives.

How the Program is Funded and How Much It Costs

♦ Most of the activities cost very little. Some extra funds may be needed for the purchase of the videotapes and audiotapes that are used in the class, but few of these costs would be beyond a normal classroom science budget. Most of the enhancements are obtained through either science education vendors who specialize in biological or science supplies, or through local stores such as grocery stores or variety stores.

Things to Consider

♦ Although the enhancements and motivating activities appear to be fairly simple, they require additional planning and, of course, classroom control. It pays to "test-run" activities and have teachers do all of the activities prior to trying them with students.

♦ All of the additional enhancements, including working with younger children require additional time; therefore, management of the pacing and scheduling of the various activities is critical to success. In most cases, the activities and enhancements take longer than originally planned.

Current Progress and Results

♦ Several achievement indicators have notably improved, including grades, attendance, and test scores. In addition, fewer problems with behavior and discipline are occurring.

- The work with younger students has helped improve cross–grade-level cooperation among students and teachers.

- Students demonstrate improved attitudes toward science and science content, and often make reference to how science is connected with their lives and interests, even though most of the students are focused on the arts.

School and Demographic Information

Roosevelt Magnet School
1704 W. Aiken Street
Peoria, IL 61605

- 800 students, grades K-8; 55 teachers; 60% African American and minority; low income; urban

Contact

Maryann Watson
1704 N. North
Peoria, IL 61604
Voice: 309-688-7415
E-mail: pakawats@aol.com

Leveling Up, Not Watering Down: The Successful Transition to Heterogeneous Grouping

Wayland Middle School, Wayland, Massachusetts

This middle school's approach to moving from tracked English and language arts classes to heterogeneously grouped classes is innovative in how it includes previously low-track students in high level, challenging, and accelerated classes. Students were regrouped into smaller classes and used a "high" course to bring students once thought to be deficient or of low-ability into the "high" class.

The Program's Goals

- ♦ To improve classroom behavior.

- ♦ To improve academic performance, especially in English and language arts courses.

How the Program Works

- ♦ Using goals for the "top" track English course, all students are placed in this course and teachers are redistributed to maintain about a 20:1 student-teacher ratio. In other words, all but the highest level course are eliminated, and all students heterogeneously placed into this course.

- ♦ A wider variety of activities and learning strategies are used in this course, and cooperative learning is used to a great extent. Each student is also independently responsible for his or her work and achievement. A rich assortment of challenging learning activities, once thought to be the purview of "gifted" courses, is used in the course.

- ♦ The lower class size allows for additional instructional time and although the work is challenging for all students, the collaborative nature of the classes helps all students reach higher levels of achievement.

♦ Resource center teachers assist regular education teachers with those students identified as being in need of additional instruction.

♦ Careful records of behavior and indicators of improved performance are kept and communicated to all interested persons in the school community.

How the Program is Funded and How Much It Costs

♦ No additional funding is needed because the net effect of rearranging the teachers was zero. That is, by redistributing students and teachers into a 20:1 ratio, no additional staff was needed. Course materials from the original "top" course were used in all classes.

Things to Consider

♦ Accurate and relevant information regarding the effects and results of tracking must be given to all teachers; an effort should be made to show how grouping of students strictly by ability is not effective. Teachers should also be deeply and meaningfully involved in the restructuring of the classes and redistribution of students.

♦ Adequate school board and administrative support is needed. The key to this appears to be showing how smaller class sizes, accelerated courses, and challenging curricula will be available to all students.

♦ Collaboration and communication with resources and other special education personnel are important.

Current Progress and Results

♦ Inappropriate behavior in class has nearly disappeared. Students are on-task to a greater extent that in the previous groupings.

♦ Academic performance improved significantly. Besides grade improvement, a number of students who were once in the lower tracks, have been recommended for "honors" courses in the high school.

♦ The strongest performances and improvements have been within the group that was formerly classified as "average" or "middle." Theses students obviously gained more from being in smaller classes than from being placed in the middle "track."

♦ Many teachers indicate that they are surprised and delighted at the substantial gains in performance by students who would have been placed in "low" tracks prior to this arrangement. They also indicate that student behavior is much better, and that the students are demonstrating higher levels of personal responsibility for learning.

School and Demographic Information

Wayland Middle School
201 Main Street
Wayland, MA 01778

♦ 650 students, grades 6–8; 50 teachers; 75% white; middle- and upper-class; suburban (urban students bused to the school)

Contact

David Summergrad
62 Green Street
Needham, MA 02192
Voice: 617-449-0012
Fax: 617-449-0012
E-mail: summergrad@eol.mass.edu

Buckeye Blockbuster— A Whole-School Interdisciplinary Project

Eastwood Middle School, Pemberville, Ohio

This innovative, thematic, integrated unit is unique in that the entire school participates. It is a good example of how an entire school faculty can build rigorous, exciting units of study that emphasize academic as well as social values. It is also innovative with respect to the overall coordination of the unit, which is done by the school's exploratory or prevocational teachers.

The Program's Goals

- ◆ To promote interest and knowledge about the State of Ohio through exploration of activities and lessons.

- ◆ To create an Ohio spirit of pride within the school.

- ◆ To familiarize students with information about Ohio and its many famous people and places.

- ◆ To provide educational knowledge and information about Ohio recreational activities, vacation spots, and historical activities.

- ◆ To improve students' awareness of the resources that are available from the State of Ohio.

How the Program Works

- ◆ For an eight-day period, students, teachers, community members, professional speakers, and local government leaders are involved in meeting the unit's goals. Each grade level (six, seven, and eight) plans and develops learning activities centered on the State of Ohio. Each team is required to include a trivia treasure hunt, guest speakers, and to have its respective team areas decorated in a manner complementary to the theme.

- The "rotation" teachers, or exploratory and prevocational teachers, coordinate and manage all aspects of the unit, as well as provide instructional activities related to the theme.

- Some of the notable activities included in the unit are:

  - A "kickoff day" that features groups of speakers about a topic, with each grade level participating in a different topic; for example, the sixth grade opening topic is about agriculture, the seventh grade topic is state history, and the eighth grade topic is technology in the state;

  - Map and geography skills, including topology, travel in the state, geology, and geological history, political areas and boundaries, and sites of interest;

  - Integrated mathematics activities;

  - A study of goods and services found in Ohio, both contemporary and historical;

  - A study of plants and animals indigenous to the area, including those that are endangered or extinct;

  - A study of medical, social, and health-related industries, history, and facilities;

  - Musical concerts and performances featuring noted Ohio composers and musicians;

  - A technological study of Ohio automobile racing including student-built cars;

  - A town meeting with local officials that focuses on issues related to residents of Ohio;

  - A study of scientists and inventors who do or did reside in Ohio

  - A biological study of fruits and vegetables, most notably the tomato (the state fruit), grown and harvested in Ohio;

  - A schoolwide quilt-making project;

  - A study of the Ohio Amish.

How the Program is Funded and How Much It Costs

♦ Each academic team receives $250 to spend on the project. In addition, a $500 grant was awarded to the school by the state middle school association to help in the purchase of materials such as computer programs, quilting materials, maps, and supplies.

♦ Speakers are paid through the principal's discretionary fund and through the student council budget.

♦ Donations of goods and services are solicited from local merchants to use as awards and prizes.

Things to Consider

♦ Start early and allow for extra time for planning and coordination.

♦ Prior to implementation a full budget should be prepared, along with funding sources; it is important for all staff to be involved in this phase of the project.

♦ Careful planning of the schedule of events is important, especially because many of the topics are covered with outside speakers and experts. Planning should take place as early as possible to allow for the greatest coordination of events.

♦ Many states have free or inexpensive resources available for schools to use in these types of units.

♦ Full support from the faculty and staff is critical; input and advice should be solicited from all areas of the school academic teachers as well as the school support staff.

♦ Design and develop assessment and evaluation methods prior to beginning the unit to measure effectiveness.

Current Progress and Results

♦ The success of the program allowed the school to continue expanding the unit.

♦ The school and the unit were featured in several educational publications.

- Students and parents were enthusiastic and supportive of the program.

- Students appear to have gained a great deal of knowledge about their home state; nationally standardized test scores, however, do not measure this.

- The overall quality of the various student-developed projects completed during the unit was very high; teachers indicated that some of the work was the best they have seen from students.

School and Demographic Information

Eastwood Middle School
4800 Sugar Ridge Road
Pemberville, OH 43450

- 450 students, grades 6–8; 30 teachers; 90%+ white; middle class; rural

Contact

Jacki Pollick or Bill McFarland
4800 Sugar Ridge Road
Pemberville, OH 43450
Voice: 419-833-6011
Fax: 419-833-7454
E-mail: eams_bac@mavca.ohio.gov

Realistic Reading

Hightower Trail Middle School, Marietta, Georgia

This unique and innovative year-long reading approach goes far beyond simple reading and decoding skills to consider workplace skills, personal citizenship, technology use, interpersonal skills, organizing and communicating information, creative and problem-solving thinking, and making decisions. To meet the program's goals, students produce a number of products useful in contemporary culture.

The Program's Goals

- ◆ To help students develop ways to become well-informed citizens.

- ◆ To help students apply reading strategies to improve learning across the curriculum.

- ◆ To help students acquire the competencies needed to describe, define, and solve problems.

- ◆ To help students identify and use the key resources that are available to them in contemporary culture and society, and to perform purposeful research of a topic.

- ◆ To help students improve personal qualities such as working with others, understanding relationships, improving self-esteem, accountability, honesty, integrity, and responsibility.

How the Program Works

- ◆ Using the newspaper *USA Today* and the free daily teaching guide that accompanies a classroom subscription to the newspaper, students are exposed to national current events. In addition, the teacher uses newspaper activities to incorporate lessons based on multiple intelligences and higher order thinking skills into the lessons.

- ◆ All areas of the curriculum are woven into the various articles presented in the newspaper. For example, geography, mathematics, science, economics, and politics can all be woven into an article about endangered species or the environment.

♦ Student work takes the form of supplemental journals that describe topics and issues throughout the year.

♦ The newspaper is used at least three times a week, and can be used flexibly; it can be used to develop a comprehensive thematic unit of study or a short lesson.

♦ In-depth information and additional resources are available by connecting to the Internet using the listings in the newspaper, teacher's guides, and student guides.

♦ Family activities throughout the year connect the learning to the home. Family nights, which often include potluck dinners, give parents the opportunity to view their student's work and accomplishments which are the result of the extensive reading.

How the Program is Funded and How Much It Costs

♦ The program is funded through the local school district and through various grants. The program has been so successful that all 18 middle schools in the school district now use this program. It is also used in the middle school summer program.

♦ Local grants and business partners may also provide funding for the materials.

Things to Consider

♦ Although the program is commercially produced, it has been proven to be very successful with diverse students. Consider applying for local grants to fund the program and keep close track of students' reading skills and scores.

♦ Workshops are available from *USA Today* to assist planners and implementers of the program.

Current Progress and Results

♦ Reading skills as well as interest in reading grew and improved.

♦ Students consistently report enthusiasm and interest in current events.

- Students report that their improved knowledge of world and national events has had a positive impact on their self-esteem.

- Teachers report improved reading skills as well as higher test scores.

- Parents report that students are asking them to subscribe to more newspapers.

- Student journals and other writing indicate a wider, more thorough understanding of complex social issues.

- Parents report that their children are reading for pleasure at home more often than prior to the implementation of this program.

School and Demographic Information

Hightower Trail Middle School
3905 Post Oak Tritt Rd.
Marietta, GA 30062

- 1,050 students, grades 6–8; 70 teachers; 90% white; middle class; suburban

Contact

Ilene Abrams
938 New Bedford Dr.
Marietta, GA 30068
Voice: 770-998-8385

The National Student Research Center

Mandeville Middle School, Mandeville, Louisiana

Too often middle school students see little application or relevance to their work. This innovative program links student learning, especially in the areas of science and literacy, in a national, as well as locally, pertinent way. Students participate in thoughtful and meaningful research and higher order thinking using technology and the NSRC's electronic school district housed on the Internet.

The Program's Goals

♦ To promote scientific literacy, science process kills, technological proficiency, higher order thinking, and language arts skills in an integrated fashion.

♦ To connect all subject areas in meaningful ways for students.

♦ To help students become humanitarians and ecologically responsible citizens.

♦ To improve students' awareness of the diverse global community.

How the Program Works

♦ Student Research Centers are located in hundreds of schools across the country and are connected by the NSRC's Internet School District and libraries of student research (http://members.aol.com/nsrcmms/NSRC.html).

♦ The basic learning approach uses the following approaches and strategies toward student experimental research that includes both qualitative and quantitative methods:

  • Students form cooperative research teams, usually of four members, at local, national, and international levels using the NSRC's electronic school district;

- Students choose a topic of study in which they have a personal interest; the topic is usually connected to a thematic unit of study taking place in the schools;

- Student teams complete a Scientific Research Contract;

- Student teams write a statement of purpose and complete a thorough review of the literature related to the topic;

- Students construct a hypothesis regarding the topic and develop methodology using control and experimental groups in which the dependent and independent variables are clearly stated; a list of materials needed to conduct the research and a data collection form are also developed;

- Students spend two to three weeks conducting the study, engaging in experiments, making observations, and recording data systematically on the forms previously developed;

- Students compile the data using computer-generated graphs, charts, and tables;

- Students analyze the data and either accept or reject their respective hypotheses;

- Students write a formal summary and conclusion regarding the project and then form a committee that will generate ways to apply the information and research they have gathered;

- The teams conduct a formal presentation of their project to a school audience, which presentation is videotaped so that others can review the project;

- The students write an abstract of their research that can be published in a local scientific journal or a nationally circulated journal of student research published by NSRC;

- Students use computers to desktop publish their research and then distribute the research locally and throughout the school community.

- Students may also conduct survey research (attitudes, opinions, etc.) that follows a similar format, but instead of using a science concept or principle, students conduct survey research related to a local or global issue of similar relevant magnitude. Students construct and use questionnaires that can be administered both locally and nationally through the NSRC Electronic School District. Much like the scientific studies, students gather, analyze, and present the results of their study.

♦ The writing processes and products completed are edited and examined by both peers and teachers, and extensive writing instruction takes place during the process.

How the Program is Funded and How Much It Costs

♦ Program materials for school use are distributed by the National Student Research Center at no cost to schools. There is no charge for national publication of student research. Costs associated with publications of student research at the local level are minimal and usually within the local budgetary limits.

♦ Although not completely necessary, additional equipment such as computers, Internet access, modems, printers, scanners, and software is useful. However, the program can take place with minimal equipment and software.

Things to Consider

♦ Planning is essential and a thoroughly developed set of procedures is needed prior to implementation.

♦ Assistance is available from NSRC (see its Web site address above).

Current Progress and Results

♦ At Mandeville, the approach has been empirically examined for several years. Results indicate that:

• Student enthusiasm for science as measured by the number and quality of student projects has risen dramatically. The number of projects has increased from about 40 in 1987 to over 1,000 in recent years;

• Science achievement as measured by the California Achievement Test (CAT) has increased by over 60 points;

• Students completing projects demonstrate significant increases in overall cognitive skills and higher order thinking skills;

- Students completing projects show significant gains in language arts skills over those students who did not complete projects.

School and Demographic Information

Mandeville Middle School
2525 Soult Street
Mandeville, LA 70448

♦ 1,100 students, grades 4–6; 80 teachers/staff; 93% white; middle class; suburban

Contact

John I. Swang
Mandeville Middle School
2525 Soult Street
Mandeville, LA 70448
Voice: 504-626-5980 or 504-626-8778
Fax: 504-626-1640
E-mail: nsrcmms@aol.com
School home page: http://members.aol.com/nsrcmms/NSRC.html

TEAMS:
Technology Enhancing Achievement in Middle School

Institute for School Innovation, Florida State University, Tallahassee, Florida

This program is currently in place in four Florida middle schools and is very successful in meeting its goal. It is unique in the way it incorporates technology and learning stations into thematic, interdisciplinary instruction across four disciplines.

The Program's Goals

♦ To enhance academic achievement through technology integration, active learning, and interdisciplinary connections.

How the Program Works

♦ This model is comprised of four nine-week thematic units that integrate the four major subject content areas. During the nine weeks, students engage in several rotations to learn the specific content and skills related to the unit theme. Each rotation period takes between 8 and 12 days and begins with whole-group instruction and moves to small, cooperative groups as the students learn the skills and content.

♦ Once students have completed the rotation, they work at learning stations for four to six days to practice and extend the teacher-led content, using multiple learning modalities. Each class is divided into four cooperative groups, with each group assigned a particular station each day. The four stations are a "Technology Station" for computer-based learning, two "Exploration Stations" for creative and game-like activities, and a "Text Station" for written and composing work. Students typically spend one class period at each station.

♦ After completing the station work, there is a whole-group reflective lesson that is used to discuss and review what has been learned about the theme, followed by individual testing and assessment.

♦ There are also nonacademic theme-based units taking place during this period, during which students explore personal development issues and themes.

How the Program is Funded and How Much It Costs

♦ The materials and training are available from the Institute for School Innovation and include teacher planning guides and student work logs. The cost for year-long training and a full set of materials for 4 teachers and 175 students in four subjects is $8,600. Renewal materials cost about $2,100 per year.

♦ Each classroom also needs to be equipped with at least four computers with appropriate software.

Things to Consider

♦ Teacher planning and collaboration, which should take place at least once a week, are crucial for the success of the program.

♦ It is sometimes difficult for teachers to move into a more facilitative role, especially during the time students are at the learning stations.

♦ Substantial time is needed for teachers to develop station activities and to become fully familiar with the subject-oriented software. Therefore, TEAMS teachers must be hardworking and flexible, with a strong understanding and appreciation of the preadolescent child.

♦ Some students may initially have difficulty adjusting to the responsibility and goal-directed behavior necessary for success in a TEAMS classroom. However, with proper training and patience, these students quickly learn to follow the procedures for self-directed learning.

♦ It is important for the TEAMS teachers to have strong instructional leadership from a building principal who can also assist in the provision of the necessary equipment and materials, as well as the time needed for teacher planning.

Current Progress and Results

- Student and teacher attitudes about learning and school are noticeably and measurably improved where the TEAMS process is used.

- Academic improvement is most likely in schools fully implementing the TEAMS process.

- Higher levels of academic success are more likely if the middle school student came from an elementary school with a strong technology component.

School and Demographic Information

Institute for School Innovation
Florida State University
PO Box 13296
Tallahassee, FL 32317-3296

- The TEAMS program is in place in four middle schools in Florida, all of which have high proportion of low SES students and significant minority populations.

Contact

Sally Butzin
Institute for School Innovation
PO Box 13296
Tallahassee, FL 32317-3296
Voice: 850-385-6985
E-mail: staff@ifsi.org
Home page: www.ifsi.org

Assessment

These are unique approaches to assessments that include ways to more authentically measure learning and skills development:

Portfolios: Middle School Dreamcatchers: Mount View Middle School (Maryland)

> Portfolios are used comprehensively to assess several subjects and student learning objectives, and are linked with student performances and demonstrations

Reading/Writing Portfolios for 6th, 7th, and 8th Graders: Lawrence Middle School (New York)

> Students take an active role in their own assessment throughout the year, and portfolio grades and evaluations are used to determine grades and ratings

Co-NECT Design: Scott Middle School (Indiana)

> This is a comprehensive approach that uses multiage groups, project-based learning, authentic and traditional types of grading and evaluation, and a great deal of technology

Science Write-ups for Middle Grade Students: Charlotte Country Day School (North Carolina)

> Instructional science education strategy used across four grade-levels that builds on each year's accomplishments and skills development

Mission Most Probable: Lake Braddock Secondary School (Virginia)

> Strong planning and organization help link student technology objectives and standards with academic subject matter objectives and standards

Portfolios: Middle School Dreamcatchers

Mount View Middle School, Marriottsville, Maryland

Mount View's approach to a comprehensive, consistent, portfolio process for student assessment and reflection is innovative in how it uses all teachers in all subject areas, including the related arts teachers. The process is also unique in the way students present their portfolios and recognize their individual learning and growth throughout their middle school years.

The Program's Goals

- ◆ To improve students' achievement and their ability to reflect on their yearly achievement and learning.

- ◆ To help teachers across grades and disciplines to recognize student growth.

- ◆ To help students recognize the value of schooling and schoolwork and build pride and self-esteem.

How the Program Works

- ◆ Representatives of all of the teachers in the school, including those in related arts, developed a consistent procedure for the collection, assessment, and evaluation of student work, including timelines for reflection and presentations, forms of achievement to be included in the portfolios, and the manner work would be evaluated.

- ◆ Each team developed a method for storing and organizing student work and shared their respective procedures with other teachers in the building.

- ◆ Throughout the school year, students on each team collect and organize their accomplishments and work in all of their subject areas. Each student is asked to think about the topics and skills they are learning, and to present their work in a manner that demonstrates both understanding of the content and the skills associated with it.

Students are encouraged to include work that shows marked improvement in an area as well as high quality work.

♦ Near the end of May, students are given several hours during the school day to evaluate the year's work and plan a personal presentation based on their portfolio collections.

♦ Students give their respective presentations during advisory period (homeroom) to their peers, thus keeping the groups relatively small and assuring the inclusion of the related arts teachers who also have advisory groups. The presentations often include areas in which students identified weaknesses or lack of understanding and how they grew and overcame these weaknesses throughout the year.

♦ Students, as they leave the eighth grade and move on to high school, will leave the middle school with a well-organized portfolio that documents their success and accomplishments during their stay in the middle school and which will provide high school teachers with a good look at how a student has progressed.

How the Program is Funded and How Much It Costs

♦ Little additional money is necessary, except for the purchase of storage containers in which to store and organize student work. Mount View spent about $500 for these containers.

Things to Consider

♦ The process of gathering and maintaining teachers' commitment to such a comprehensive project is critical to its success. It is best to spend a great deal of planning time and faculty meeting time discussing the various advantages and disadvantages of the process, as well as overcoming objections and problem solving.

♦ Managing the logistics of sorting and organizing a large volume of student work can be difficult; it is important to make appropriate accommodations and plans to keep this part of the process from posing difficulties for teachers and students. It is perhaps best to allow each team to make these arrangements.

♦ Consistency in terms of assessment processes is also critical. Students and teachers alike should have a clear understanding of the assessment criteria as well as the levels of quality that will be presented.

♦ This kind of process, especially one as comprehensive and complex as this, takes several years of planning, changing, and refining before many of the problems are eliminated or solved; be prepared to spend several years refining the process.

Current Progress and Results

♦ Teachers have indicated a greater awareness of the progress of their own students and the progress of those on other teams.

♦ Students are more aware of their progress and the learning taking place in the school.

♦ Teachers continue to refine and improve the process as new ways to organize, assess, and present student materials are discovered.

School and Demographic Information

Mount View Middle School
12101 Woodford Drive
Marriottsville, MD 21104

♦ 600 students, grades 6–8; 40 teachers; 86% white; middle- and upper-class; rural/suburban

Contact

Susan Berrington
Mount View Middle School
12101 Woodford Drive
Marriottsville, MD 21104
Voice: 410-313-5545
Fax: 410-313-5551
E-mail: sberrington@ccentral.howard.k12.md.us

Reading/Writing Portfolios for 6th, 7th, and 8th Graders

Lawrence Middle School, Lawrence, New York

Lawrence Middle School's use of reading and writing portfolios is unique in several ways: the portfolios are used to assess and demonstrate writing proficiencies and growth over a full school year, are assessed on a very regular basis with students taking part in the assessment process, and are used as a significant portion of students' final examination grades.

The Program's Goals

♦ To provide an authentic assessment tool that is largely student driven.

♦ To provide students with the opportunity to view and reflect on their personal learning and growth.

How the Program Works

♦ For several summers, teachers worked to select, adapt, and develop a portfolio process that fit the school and its students well, that was research-based and focused on authentic assessment procedures and alternatives, and that was manageable. The school-based portfolio process was an outgrowth of earlier district efforts to create comprehensive reading and writing folders for students.

♦ At the beginning of the school year, the school's teachers administer an interest inventory survey to gather information about their students' personal interests.

♦ During the same period, teachers conduct one-on-one conferences with their students to help students develop good learning goals for themselves and to help guide students toward district and state outcomes.

♦ Most student work is compiled in their respective portfolios, and at the end of ten weeks each student assesses his or her progress toward writing goals; in addition, students list the reading that they have accomplished during the period and choose one exemplary piece of writing to retain in their portfolios, stating why the particular piece was chosen.

♦ At the end of the school year, students are guided to write a formal essay that describes their growth as readers and writers. Each student also has a formal reading/writing conference with his or her teacher that examines the student's learning, growth, and skills. A descriptive rubric with criteria is used to grade the portfolio and this grade is used as 50% of the student's final examination grade for the year.

How the Program is Funded and How Much It Costs

♦ Funds were obtained from the school district to support the portfolio development processes, including funding for substitute teachers at the end of the school year to cover classes while the teachers conferred with their students about the portfolios. Other costs for the program are minimal.

Things to Consider

♦ Initial parent communication is extremely important, especially when considering the use of the portfolio as 50% of a student's final examination grade.

♦ Ongoing communication with parents is important to ensure ongoing parental support for the project.

♦ The process should be carefully examined to make sure that the skills the students are developing are consistent with future high school testing processes, especially if the state has high-stakes testing barriers in place.

♦ It is important to gain as much internal or departmental teacher support and input as possible to retain the commitment to the process.

Current Progress and Results

♦ Initially, only seventh- and eighth-grade portfolio processes were put in place; currently the process for the sixth grade students is based on the same premise, but the processes and procedure have been somewhat simplified.

♦ The use of portfolios is well established and accepted in both classrooms and by parents.

♦ All students, regardless of ability or exceptionality, have portfolios in which they have a great deal of pride and that provide clear evidence of learning and growth.

♦ The use of this authentic assessment process is being emphasized as the method in which students may be evaluated or assessed later in life.

School and Demographic Information

Lawrence Middle School
195 Broadway
Lawrence, NY 11559

♦ 900 students, grades 6–8; 80 staff and teachers; very diverse; suburban (New York City)

Contact

Vicki Karant
Lawrence Middle School
195 Broadway
Lawrence, NY 11559
Voice: 516-295-7016

Co-NECT Design

Scott Middle School, Hammond, Indiana

The innovative approach to education described below is unique in its comprehensive approach. It is a total school program that uses multiage grouping of students, project-based learning activities, authentic as well as traditional approaches to evaluation, and a high degree of technology. After only two years, the school has had a great deal of success.

The Program's Goals

♦ To provide students with challenging school work, connections to real life, an engaging and exciting curriculum, and a desire for life-long learning.

♦ To provide teachers with technology expertise, teamwork skills, and an expanded repertoire of teaching strategies.

♦ To provide the community with a school that meets the academic, social, and career needs of children and parents.

How the Program Works

♦ This whole-school program uses a variety of innovative structural as well as teaching strategies.

♦ Students are grouped in multiage teams across all three grade levels. Teachers remain with the same students over the three years in order to develop a "family-like" team culture that is based on nurturing growth as well as academic achievement. Older students on the teams, as well as the teachers, welcome and nurture the younger students as they progress through the school year.

♦ Teams of teachers as well as students and other community members work collaboratively to develop a sequence of projects for students to complete throughout the year. The themes for the projects are those that are of local interest and value, and that have intrinsic and extrinsic value for students and teachers. Academic rigor and skills instruction are included in natural settings as students progress through the projects; students see school work as "real" work as the projects have local significance, application, and relevance to student lives.

♦ Extensive use of technology and technological tools are evident, including computers, software, video facilities, and the Internet. Teachers and students are extensively trained in the use of various technologies and the students' projects rely heavily on technological use and expertise.

♦ Challenging standards have been set for student work that is assessed and evaluated both in authentic and more traditional ways. Grading scales and rubrics have been developed to assess student work and these instruments are used to communicate learning and achievement to parents and the community.

How the Program is Funded and How Much It Costs

♦ Initial funds to retrofit the school for the necessary technology were provided by the local school district. These costs will vary from school to school.

♦ Funds to purchase computer hardware were provided by a grant from the New American Schools Development Corporation. Funds for hardware will also vary from school to school.

♦ Little other additional funding is needed to implement the program.

Things to Consider

♦ Whenever an organization deviates from traditional approaches in education, there can be resistance and difficulties.

♦ The school staff and faculty need to be very well organized, hardworking, and committed to the program.

♦ Teachers will need staff development and training in order to move away from traditional text-oriented teaching toward these new approaches.

♦ The faculty will need to be composed of visionary individuals who are not afraid to take well-planned professional risks.

♦ School administrators need to be supportive and committed to the process.

♦ Schools planning to follow this format will need to make extensive plans several years prior to implementing the program, including plans to improve technology in the school.

Current Progress and Results

♦ After only two years experience with the program, the school is experiencing a number of improvements, most notably:

- Improved attendance by both students and faculty;

- Improved student enthusiasm for school—students are excited about coming to school;

- Students indicate an expanded and enhanced view of how what they do in school relates to the world outside of home and school;

- Student accomplishments are seen as relevant and rewarding for students, parents, and teachers;

- Standardized test scores are improving.

School and Demographic Information

Scott Middle School
3635 173rd Street
Hammond, IN 46323

♦ 660 students, grades 6–8; 45 teachers; 70% white; low- to middle-class; medium-sized urban

Contact

Frank Lentvorsky
Scott Middle School
3635 173rd St.
Hammond, IN 46323
Voice: 219-989-7340
Fax: 219-989-7342
E-mail: lentvorf@hammond.k12.in.us
School home page: http://www.hammond.k12.in.us/scottms.html

Science Write-ups for Middle Grade Students

Charlotte Country Day School, Charlotte, North Carolina

This innovative instructional strategy combines a number of consistent science process skills across four grade levels. As students progress through the grades, the processes become more complex and rigorous, and build on what students have learned in previous grades. Students use various scientific classroom roles throughout the grades and use technology and good writing skills in truly effective ways.

The Program's Goals

♦ To use a consistent, scientifically sound method of developing scientific process skills across grade levels.

♦ To use technology and writing skills in scientifically thoughtful and meaningful ways.

♦ To integrate other subjects into science when appropriate.

♦ To encourage and motivate students to use higher order thinking skills.

How the Program Works

♦ Beginning in the fifth grade of this K-12 school, all students are taught to use a process of writing and thinking in science classes that is founded on the Cornell note style.

♦ The basic format of the style includes:

• Title (written by the teacher);

• Purpose (written by the teacher);

• Hypothesis—in fifth grade, students are introduced to the formation of hypotheses and how to phrase them; in sixth grade, students write their own hypotheses, and in seventh and eighth grade, students write more sophisticated hypotheses that include conditions and variables;

- Materials (provided by the teacher);

- Data—all data that are measured or examined in the science lab are included; tables and spreadsheet applications are used to organize data;

- Analysis—scientific and statistical comparisons and evaluations are completed by the students; at each grade level, the analyses become more sophisticated and thorough, integrating math concepts into the procedures;

- Conclusions—in the fifth grade, students are asked to answer various questions about the scientific concepts being studied, rather than forming conclusions; in the sixth grade, students write conclusions based on their experiments and observations; in the seventh grade, students present more fully developed conclusions that relate results to hypotheses, establish relationships among variables, and address key scientific concepts, critiquing the lab with a focus on experimental error; in the eighth grade, students concentrate on designing data tables and analysis sections of the write-ups that are related to refined, concrete conclusions.

♦ A fully developed, thorough evaluation rubric or grading scale is used at each grade level that is consistent with the write-up format. Each section noted above is completely described in the rubric, with grade scales and evaluations thoroughly described for each item.

♦ Other subjects such as English and language arts, social studies, and mathematics are integrated throughout the year as appropriate.

How the Program is Funded and How Much It Costs

♦ There are no additional costs associated with the program.

Things to Consider

♦ The use of a well-developed rubric is essential to the success of the process. As students progress through the grades, they are familiar with the process and the rubric.

♦ It is also essential that the process be used throughout all of the grade levels. It is a fairly complex process that needs consistent application and use.

♦ Teacher planning and coordination across grade levels are crucial if the process is to be used consistently.

Current Progress and Results

♦ Student achievement in science has improved to a large extent, especially in the areas most critical for scientific thinking: hypothesizing, analyzing, comparing, looking for experimental errors, and drawing sound conclusions.

♦ At the end of the eighth grade, students have a much deeper understanding and more thorough knowledge of scientific concepts and processes.

♦ Writing has improved for all students, especially in the areas of composition and clarity.

♦ The high school teachers have noted increased comprehension of scientific concepts and higher order thinking in all subjects.

School and Demographic Information

Charlotte Country Day School
1440 Carmel Road
Charlotte, NC 28226

♦ 500 students, grades 5–8 (1600 total school population); 300+ teachers and staff; 89% white; middle-class; suburban

Contact

Jennifer Hinote
6724 Alexander Road
Charlotte, NC 28270
Voice: 704-362-6724
Fax: 704-367-1174
E-mail: hinote@over.ccds.charlotte.nc.us

Mission Most Probable

Lake Braddock Secondary School, Burke, Virginia

Lake Braddock's seventh grade team's interdisciplinary approach to meeting technology standards and academic objectives is indicative of how technology skills are less a separate subject than tools for learning. The way this program aligns the two is unique and unusual, and demonstrates a great deal of comprehensive planning about technology and subject-matter content.

The Program's Goals

- To help the school meet the state's mandated technology standards for students.

- To demonstrate how computers and technology are tools to help students explore and learn about historical developments in science and technology as well as to learn core academic concepts.

How the Program Works

- This seventh grade team approached the task of meeting technology skills objectives for students and subject-matter objectives as an exercise in developing integrated, thematic instructional units. They began by subdividing and placing the technology objective areas (applications software, network communications and home page development, data storage and retrieval, and information and research retrieval) into naturally fitting applications within the four core subject areas. Investigation topics as well as skills development fell under the umbrella topic of "Our Future." Examples of the applications and investigations are:

  - Mathematics: spreadsheets and graphing calculators, data analysis, random numbers for simulations, functions of change;

  - Science: Web page development, research into alternative energy resources, development of imaginary city;

  - History: database development for historic facts and events, research and investigations into technological disasters, impact of technology on society, need for new inventions and technologies;

- English: writing skills, literature investigations through the Internet, and writing and research about technological applications related to medicine and health.

♦ In addition to the content and technology skills built into the instructional unit, the team incorporated activities designed to address students' different and multiple intelligences, cooperative learning, and learning styles.

How the Program is Funded and How Much It Costs

♦ No additional funds are needed for this program, but much additional time is necessary. Parent volunteers are also needed to assist with many of the individual projects and technology applications.

Things to Consider

♦ For many schools, access to computers and the Internet pose problems. It is important to plan these activities far enough in advance to assure access to technology.

♦ Assessment is critical to the success of this sort of problem; assessment of student progress toward objectives should include both academic subject assessments and technology skills assessment.

Current Progress and Results

♦ Nearly all (98%) of the students on the team have demonstrated mastery of spreadsheet applications including data organization and arithmetic operations.

♦ All students had experience and exposure to Web-based and other (CD-ROM) research processes.

♦ A majority of students demonstrated mastery understanding of evaluation of Web pages for research use.

♦ All students have mastered database organization and applications.

School and Demographic Information

Lake Braddock Secondary School
9200 Burke Lake Road
Burke, VA 22015

♦ Grade 7 team: 125 students; 20% minority; low- to middle-income; suburban

Contact

Chris Mackmin
7771 Turlock Road
Springfield, VA 22153
Voice: 703-451-9014
E-mail: revelry@.com

3

At-risk Students, Behavior, and Motivation

Every middle school teacher and administrator has heard "how can you stand those kids?" at one time or another in their professional lives. The perception about middle level students that these sorts of comments lead us to is that students at this age all fit the same mold—one that seems to suggest that middle school children are disrespectful, lazy, unmotivated, loud, obnoxious, and are seen only in packs in shopping malls. Nothing could be further from the truth. Middle school-aged children are intensely interested in what adults have to say and what they do. They are often hypercritical of adult behavior as they try to sort out what is right and what is wrong. Their changing bodies subject them to periods of high energy and periods of listlessness and sleepiness, and often they are not comfortable sitting in what we might consider a proper position. They are motivated by their curiosity and their confused but energetic attempts at making sense of their world. And it is true that the vast majority of middle school-aged children make it successfully through this period.

But it is equally true that for many children this period of life can bring about an awareness of the unfairness of life, of how certain groups in our culture remain oppressed, of how hopeless a future life can seem. Nearly one-fourth of our nation's children live at or below the poverty line. Middle school students are keenly aware of the material things that the culture says are necessary for happiness—for many it is the first time in their lives that they have adultlike choices to make. Many of them have not yet developed good nutritional habits, and many are far from being in shape physically. They must decide to work hard in school or to simply play the school game until something better comes along. They must choose whether or not to engage in sexual behaviors—a difficult choice given their changing bodies and the attention our culture gives to sex. They must choose to avoid drugs and dangerous substances or to leave them alone. It can be, and often is, a challenging, difficult period of life, and the term "at-risk" has more meaning for middle schoolers than for any other group, because it is during these years that these critical choices are made.

Schools have extremely important roles to play in helping children make good decisions and make proper choices. Teachers and other school personnel can be critically important—showing the children love, compassion, and care when these are often missing from children's lives outside of school. And this must be done while continuing to work toward academic achievement and skill development.

Middle schools, when clearly focused on children and the lives of children, often address these issues through a number of programmatic and structural options. Teacher advisory programs help students and teachers work toward making good choices and learning about the life period they are experiencing. Advisories also help with skill development, especially study skills, test-taking skills, and other academic needs; advisories offer students at least one adult in the school with whom they can talk or identify. Advisory programs often provide advocacy and support when little of either can be found outside of the school.

But advisory programs are very difficult programs for schools to operate—some say they are the most difficult middle school program element to do well. Advisories are difficult because teachers must take on somewhat of a different role—teachers must add another set of plans to their already overburdened jobs; schedules must be adjusted to assure time availability; teachers must be trained to use new materials and perhaps assess and evaluate students without using traditional grades or methods; and it is easy for advisory programs to deteriorate into "study halls" or time for students to socialize.

Excellent advisory programs, alternative programs, and extracurricular programs, however, can be implemented, as this chapter demonstrates. The chapter is divided into three parts, each dealing with slightly different approaches toward engaging children in school, achievement, and school life. In the first part are wonderful, innovative approaches to student health, student recognition, changing student behavior, providing alternative ways for students to be academically successful, avoiding drug and substance abuse, and helping students change violent behavior.

In the second part are programs that help students make better use of time, participate in games, sports, and other activities, and continue learning. In this era of growing demands on teachers' and administrators' time, these well-managed programs can help us deal with many of the issues and problems in schools that detract from our mission.

In the last part are four excellent advisory programs that have good track records, and that are committed to helping students meet the demands of life head-on, make good choices, and be successful.

At-risk Students, Behavior, and Motivation

These programs focus on student health, student recognition, changing student behavior, providing alternative ways for students to be academically successful, avoiding drugs and substance abuse, and helping students change violent behavior:

Healthy Bodies, Healthy Minds: School–Community-Linked Health Facility: Roosevelt Middle (Oklahoma)

> A community agency-based health facility located at the school site and managed through a unique partnership with several local agencies and organizations

Show Off; Showcasing Student Achievement: Spratley Middle (Virginia)

> A creative recognition program that combines school achievement and accomplishments with the local 4-H Fair where student work is judged against itself and not against other students' work

Sexual Harassment: Unwelcome, Unwanted, and Unsolicited: Challenger Middle (CO)

> A three-year focus on sexual harassment throughout the school where behaviors are examined and addressed in a developmentally appropriate manner

In-School Suspension: "BIP"—Behavior Improvement Program: Guilford Middle (North Carolina)

> In-school suspension program that is linked positively to consequences, academic successes, and behavior improvement that is creatively managed and coordinated

"Scorpions"—To Be or Not To Be: Conflict Mediation Through Literature: Knox Middle (Indiana)

> A schoolwide conflict mediation program that uses moral and behavioral dilemmas found in children's literature to help students see behavioral implications

Modifying the Curriculum for Adolescents Enrolled in an Alternative Program for Disruptive Youth: Neumann School (Illinois)

> Alternative school for nonspecial education students that uses alternative learning strategies including the theory of multiple intelligences, individualized instruction, and skill mastery

Second Step: A Violence Prevention Curriculum for Middle School and Junior High School: Washington Irving Middle (California)

> A strong, centralized curriculum that includes extensive parent involvement and training, coordinated programs, and integrated subjects

Supporting At-Risk Students: Ellicott Mills Middle (Maryland)

> Extensive program that includes not only intensive school-based interventions and assistance, but cooperation and coordination with the local community

World of Work—Mathematics for At-Risk Students: Stewart Middle (Virginia)

> Special education students who have difficulty with mathematics are given opportunities to work in real-life settings with the school's business partners

Programs for Student Learning: How to Think Big with Small Resources: George Washington Carver Middle (Mississippi)

> Before-school and after-school programs that are closely connected to the local housing authority to help academically struggling students

Project Alert: Best Foundation (California)

> A skills-based, long-term motivational curriculum to help middle school students avoid substance abuse, that is based on social influences and frank discussion

Healthy Bodies, Healthy Minds: School-Community-Linked Health Facility

Roosevelt Middle School, Oklahoma City, Oklahoma

Several national reports suggest that middle schools should be more closely tied to community health programs and agencies. This middle school's innovative approach to linking healthcare facilities and agencies with students and their families has helped the school address a number of health-related problems before they became serious or detrimental to student success.

The Program's Goals

♦ To provide for the mental and physical health of middle schools students, their parents, siblings, and others in the immediate school community.

How the Program Works

♦ The school-based community health facility, located at the school site, operates as a school district-managed partnership with the State Department of Health and the Youth Services for Oklahoma City agency.

♦ A nurse practitioner and a counselor are located full-time at the facility. Under the supervision of a physician, the nurse may prescribe certain medications and may also provide certain forms of medical treatment.

How the Program is Funded and How Much It Costs

♦ The program is funded by in-kind contributions from the three partner-entities. In the near future, a healthcare provider will also assume much of the cost for the services and will process third-party billing procedures when applicable.

Things to Consider

- A carefully designed study of community needs should precede implementation to accurately determine the types of services needed.

- The partnership arrangement needs to be collaborative; that is, the focus needs to remain on providing healthcare for students and their families.

Current Progress and Results

- Community support for the program has been very strong and community use of the facility has been ongoing.

- In a large number of instances, healthcare facility personnel have been able to identify and intervene in health-related cases that previously would have gone unnoticed or hidden for long periods of time.

- School children attending the school have, in many cases, attained a level of healthcare and attention they had not experienced prior to this time.

School and Demographic Information

Roosevelt Middle School
3233 S.W. 44
Oklahoma City, OK 73119

- 800+ students, grades 6–8; 60 teachers; 45% white, 55% minority; 80%+ free and reduced lunch; large urban

Contact

Dr. Ronald Maxfield
3233 S.W. 44
Oklahoma City, OK 73119
Voice: 405-685-7795

Show Off: Showcasing Student Achievement

Spratley Middle School, Hampton, Virginia

It is often difficult to motivate middle school students. It is sometimes equally difficult to find ways to meaningfully recognize exceptional student work without placing students in an awkward social position with respect to their peers. This creative recognition program combines the local 4-H Fair with recognition of student work in an exploratory class. It is also innovative in the way in which the student products are judged—the judges use the Danish Modified System of judging that assesses student work individually and not against others' work.

The Program's Goals

♦ To highlight coursework and achievements accomplished in the Work and Family Studies elective course.

♦ To increase awareness and attractiveness of the Work and Family Studies Course.

♦ To help students perceive the relevance of work accomplished in the Work and Family Studies course.

♦ To improve student awareness of the interdisciplinary nature of the curriculum.

♦ To help students build self-esteem without using competition, or win-lose events, or situations.

How the Program Works

♦ Planning for the event and publicizing the Showcase begins in the fall with coordination of activities between the school and the local extension and 4-H offices. Shared responsibilities for planning and coordination are assigned at this time, and monthly meetings are scheduled.

♦ Judges are identified during the fall, and should be selected by December. All judges are expected to spend the entire day at the March showcase and to follow the judging directions carefully and thoughtfully.

♦ In January, the final preparations for the March Showcase begin. A comprehensive list of duties and responsibilities is developed, the vast majority of which are completed by the Work and Family Studies teachers. The following is a list of some of the items that must be completed:

  • Room arrangements;

  • Formal invitations to school officials, including school board members;

  • Formal invitations to community business leaders;

  • Formal invitations to parents;

  • Procure or make all of the award ribbons and trophies;

  • Arrange for refreshments (some donated, some provided by school staff);

  • Arrange for parent, student, and other volunteers to help manage the event;

  • Coordinate activities with 4-H and County Extension Officers;

  • Explain and coordinate event with other faculty members;

  • Write and distribute news release for local papers and other media;

  • Procure and arrange for teacher leaves (for planning and actual event);

  • Procure or make posters, banners, welcome signs, etc;

  • Procure decorations and flowers for rooms.

♦ On the day of the event, student work and projects are judged by the judging panel, and awards are based on the merits of the project itself, rather than being compared to the other projects. The judging panel consists of community leaders and school-business partners. Each project will receive an award of recognition, but some are chosen as nominees for the Best of Show prize.

♦ A fashion show also takes place during this event, and students model clothing they have made in classes or selected based on specified criteria.

How the Program is Funded and How Much It Costs

◆ Most of the costs associated with this event are those required for hiring substitutes to cover teacher releases for planning and the event. Material costs vary depending on the amount and type of donations that can be procured.

Things to Consider

◆ As the program and event grows in importance and recognition, so does the need for planning. It is very important to plan early, communicate regularly and effectively with the 4-H and extension officials, and procure commitments from judges and other volunteers. In addition, regular reminder communications are needed to keep participants involved and aware of program needs and changes.

◆ Administrative support, including support from the central administration is important, especially for procuring funds for teacher release time.

◆ Strong emphasis should be placed on the nature of the partnerships with 4-H and other community leaders.

◆ Strong emphasis should be placed on the academic aspects of both the event and the processes the students followed to complete their respective projects.

Current Progress and Results

◆ Nearly 300 students participated in the last event; the number of participants grows each year.

◆ The success of this event has improved the number and quality of community partnerships with the school.

◆ Each year, the quality of the student work improves, as the teachers and other project directors focus on the interdisciplinary nature of the projects and the learning that takes place.

◆ The success of the project has resulted in an interesting phenomenon—business leaders and other community individuals are requesting to be judges for the Showcase as early as August and September.

♦ The success of the event has helped bring improved notoriety to the school and the school community.

♦ Each year the number of projects that are entered in state, regional, and national competitions has risen and the number of awards associated with these competitions has increased each year.

School and Demographic Information

Spratley Middle School
339 Woodland Road
Hampton, VA 23669

♦ 1,000 students, grades 6–8; 90 staff; 60+% African American, 40% white and other; low income; small urban

Contact

Janet B. Hoffman
112 Plainfield Drive
Newport News, VA 23602-6449
Voice: 757-877-0486 or 757-850-5032
Fax: 757-850-5411

Sexual Harassment: Unwelcome, Unwanted, and Unsolicited

Challenger Middle School, Colorado Springs, Colorado

This program is unique in the way it directly and consistently addresses sexual harassment over a student's three-year tenure in the middle school. It is also different in that it goes far beyond what is commonly found in most schools; that is, the information the students receive is linked directly to exhibited behaviors as well as potential behavior that in many schools have historically been tolerated as "something kids do."

The Program's Goals

- ◆ To prepare professional faculty and staff to deliver instruction regarding sexual harassment.

- ◆ To help educators understand the necessity of protecting students and staff from sexual harassment.

- ◆ To deliver information about sexual harassment in an age-appropriate method.

How the Program Works

- ◆ On entering the sixth grade at the middle school, students are given a comprehensive presentation regarding sexual harassment that includes a great deal of discussion about the definitions of sexual harassment and its relationship to power.

- ◆ Extensive attention is given to the difference between sexual harassment and flirting and the emotional reactions that each engenders.

- ◆ Extensive attention is also paid to the differences between sexual harassment and sexual assault.

- ◆ Students and teachers discuss the behaviors and feelings associated with sexual harassment and students are given examples of various behaviors.

- The presentation is supported with statistics about student populations and sexual harassment.

- A significant focus of the presentations is how students should respond to sexual harassment.

- Follow-up presentations and discussion take place throughout the three years a student is enrolled in the school, and data are collected to keep track of the program's effectiveness.

How the Program is Funded and How Much It Costs

- There are no additional costs associated with the program; school counselors and teachers have been extensively trained.

- Due to the success of Challenger's program, other schools and school districts often request assistance and training from Challenger staff. Challenger charges a small fee to other schools and districts to deliver the training.

Things to Consider

- Training for all staff is extremely important, especially with respect to the legal variables involved with sexual harassment.

- The topic may be a sensitive one for some staff members and students, so it is important to maintain a professional presence at all times.

Current Progress and Results

- Fewer incidents of sexual harassment, especially among students, are taking place.

- Although this type of program can result in an initial increase in reported incidents, few, if any, will result in criminal or civil cases. The program's coordinators and the school's administrators can mediate resolution.

- The number of sexual harassment cases involving students has increased across the country, and many of the cases have been decided against schools and school districts because the schools had not implemented any type of prevention activity. This type of program can prevent such a loss.

School and Demographic Information

Challenger Middle School
10215 Lexington Drive
Colorado Springs, CO 80920

- 1300+ students, grades 6–8; 70 teachers; 88% white; middle- and upper-income; suburban

Contact

Rhonda Williams
18820 St. Andrews Drive
Monument, CO 80132
Voice: 719-481-4586
E-mail: rzwilliams@aol.com

In-School Suspension: "BIP"—Behavior Improvement Program

Guilford Middle School, Greensboro, North Carolina

In-school suspension programs exist in many schools across the county. Guilford's approach is innovative and unique in that the program is an extension of the regular school programs and because the program is seen as an opportunity for student assistance that is linked positively to the punitive consequences of students' disruptive actions. It is also unusual in the way the program is supplied, staffed, and assessed, as well as in the stated responsibilities of the faculty member in charge of the classroom.

The Program's Goals

♦ To link punitive measures for disruptive or inappropriate student behavior to opportunities to assist the student academically.

♦ To develop an in-school suspension program that has academic accountability as well as behavioral accountability.

♦ To maintain an in-school suspension classroom that is staffed by a qualified teacher and maintained as a fully functioning classroom.

♦ To maintain a strict but positive learning environment in which students can receive assistance with academic and study skills.

♦ To maintain an in-school suspension program that will benefit students academically, socially, and personally.

♦ To maintain an in-school program that will help deter school dropouts.

How the Program Works

♦ The ISS program is fully staffed by a full-time certified teacher who maintains the room consistently and continually. Because the teacher is there full-time, the teacher can get to know the students better, understand the problems they are having, work more closely with the students' regular teachers, and take more positive steps toward helping the students. The room is maintained with most of the supplies a student needs while attending ISS, and the teacher has all of the supplies, materials, and equipment that other teachers have in their respective rooms. In addition, the room is equipped with carrels for individual study and work. One important aspect of the room is the range and number of textbooks in the room—there is a copy of all of the textbooks in use in the school as well as a teacher's edition for each of the texts. The room also contains a computer and printer, a small copier, calculators used in classes, and assorted reference materials including a full set of an encyclopedia.

♦ The ISS teacher also performs the duties that regular teachers in the school are required to undertake, including parent conferences and referrals to special education and IEP conferences. The teacher also works closely with the other teachers in the school to insure that the teacher is knowledgeable about students' skills, needs, assignments, homework assignments, and any special needs. The teacher is also responsible for completing the extensive documentation regarding in-school suspension.

♦ "Sentences" for in-school suspension are based on a flexible system rather than a rigid set of penalties. Great care is taken to insure that the ISS assignment is one that will accomplish the academic and behavioral goals for the student. The philosophy is based on the idea that "you made a bad choice, you're not a bad kid."

How the Program is Funded and How Much It Costs

♦ Other than normal classroom expenses, the only additional cost is that of one teacher for the position. No additional funds are used to purchase materials for the ISS room.

Things to Consider

Guilford Middle School has provided a number of ideas as well as a number of *don'ts* for implementing a middle school in-school suspension program, among the *don'ts*:

♦ Don't hire an ISS teacher who has a negative attitude, whines a lot, or has a low threshold for the emotions and frustrations of others.

- Don't give the ISS teacher a major daily job such as handling school-wide attendance records and problems.

- When the ISS teacher is absent, always hire a regular substitute teacher and be sure there are comprehensive plans for the substitute.

- Don't hire a teacher who doesn't get along with other teachers.

- Don't let a backlog of students constitute a waiting list for ISS.

- Don't allow ISS students to have breaks, socialize, or do chores around the building.

- Limit the number of ISS students at one time to eight or nine.

- Don't use ISS as your only discipline program.

- Make sure the ISS room is a warm, inviting, learning environment.

- Don't think of ISS as a "holding tank" for school thugs.

- Always refer to the ISS room as a classroom—not as an office.

- Don't make ISS students fill out a lot of forms about their psyches and personal problems.

- Always have a telephone and a pager in the ISS room.

- If possible, place the ISS room near the administrative and counseling offices.

- Make sure that there is a flexible but effective method for getting assignments from teachers and for returning assignments completed by ISS students.

Current Progress and Results

- In a recent survey, the teachers at Guilford indicated extremely high levels of support for the ISS program,

- Students assigned to ISS often miss no class content or assignments during their assignment to ISS.

- Teachers indicate strong support for the ISS teacher and that teacher's consistent methods for dealing with students, parents, and administrators.

- Teachers indicate that they are very pleased with the level of academic performance of students returning to their classes from ISS.

♦ Out-of-school suspensions have decreased dramatically, and students indicate that the threat of in-school suspension often keeps them from misbehaving in school.

School and Demographic Information

Guilford Middle School
410 College Road
Greensboro, NC 27410

♦ 1335 students, grades 3–8; 89 teachers; 70% white; mostly middle class; urban/suburban

Contact

Helen B. Stone
Guilford Middle School
401 College Road
Greensboro, NC 27410
Voice: 910-316-5833
Fax: 910-316-5837

"Scorpions"—To Be or Not To Be: Conflict Mediation Through Literature

Knox Middle School, Knox, Indiana

Knox Middle School's unique approach to supporting a schoolwide conflict mediation program is to use interesting and relevant children's literature as a mechanism to bring additional emphasis on conflict in a classroom setting. The novel *Scorpions* by Walter Dean Myers provides a variety of situations and moral dilemmas through which students can view conflicts and their consequences in a nonpersonal setting, thus helping them see how conflict mediation skills and values are essential.

The Program's Goals

♦ To integrate conflict mediation into the classroom through the use of literature.

♦ To help students realize the value of good conflict mediation skills.

♦ To help students understand the pervasiveness of conflict in school classrooms and the importance of being able to manage conflict effectively.

♦ To help students understand the conflict cycle and how conflict operates in life.

♦ To help students improve and enhance a conflict mediation program

How the Program Works

♦ Using *Scorpions* as a centerpiece of a language arts unit, the regular classroom teacher guides discussions about both the book's literary values and objectives and the many instances of internal and external conflict that are portrayed in the book.

♦ A series of well-designed lessons help students focus on the many aspects of conflict, including verbal and body language and their importance in recognizing conflicts. In addition, a great deal of emphasis is placed on the idea of individual perspective; that is, how one situation or circumstance can be viewed very differently by different people, depending on their background, experiences, and other personal factors.

♦ The school counselor, who is a trained conflict mediator, enters the sequence of lessons as the students gain understanding of these concepts.

♦ The counselor leads the students through a number of exercises designed to teach some of the skills needed to effectively mediate conflict and manage conflict resolution. Included in these activities are role plays, simulations, direct instruction, and other activities constructed to make relevant linkages between the situations in the book and situations that occur in schools and classrooms.

♦ Students are also given a written test that measures items from both the novel and conflict mediation skills lessons.

How the Program is Funded and How Much It Costs

♦ Few costs are associated with the program, but it is essential that at least one person on the team be trained as a conflict mediator. Costs associated with this training vary widely. Small grants can also be used to provide funding for this training.

Things to Consider

♦ Some teachers may not be convinced of the importance of this type of classroom process and may resist implementation. In this case, it is wise to allow them to elect not to participate but to keep emphasizing the positive results.

♦ Presenting this type of content (conflict mediation) within the confines of another content area (language arts or literature) takes additional time; careful planning and coordination are necessary to ensure the best use of time.

♦ Keep careful records of conflicts in the school and how these conflicts are resolved to measure the effectiveness of the program and the training.

♦ Administrative support is critical to assist with any scheduling problems that might arise and to help with program support and implementation.

Current Progress and Results

♦ Students consistently indicate greater awareness of daily conflict and the need to manage and resolve conflicts.

♦ The number of discipline referrals have dropped significantly since the implementation of the program.

♦ The number of violent responses to conflict (fighting) has dropped considerably with the majority of conflicts being sent to conflict mediators for resolution.

♦ Conflict mediation training within the school has been broadened and is in its third year of implementation.

School and Demographic Information

Knox Middle School
901 Main Street
Knox, IN 46534

♦ 510 students, grades 6–8; 34 teachers; 93% white; mostly low income; rural

Contact

Kathleen Kephart or Harriet Liechty
Knox Middle School
901 Main Street
Knox, IN 46534
Voice: 219-772-4555
Fax: 219-772-4438

Modifying the Curriculum for Adolescents Enrolled in an Alternative Program for Disruptive Youth

Neumann School, Chicago, Illinois

This grades 6–12 program has been very successful with students who have been unsuccessful with our traditional schooling model. It is unique in three ways: it uses the Theory of Multiple Intelligences to develop and plan individualized instruction; its students do not meet the criteria for special education services; and it is highly successful.

The Program's Goals

- ♦ To ensure academic success for students.

- ♦ To provide a functional curriculum that will provide students the opportunity to earn credit.

- ♦ To establish student skills that will enhance vocational abilities and opportunities.

How the Program Works

- ♦ The vast majority of students in this school have been expelled from school and have experienced continuous school failure.

- ♦ Students who are accepted to the school are evaluated and assessed to identify strengths, weaknesses, and the ways in which they are intelligent. Each student must meet the state minimum competencies for high school graduation; therefore, an individual learning plan is designed that will help him or her reach the necessary academic competencies and skills.

- ♦ The curriculum and instruction in all grades and subjects are modified, planned, and delivered to take advantage of students' multiple intelligences.

How the Program is Funded and How Much It Costs

- No additional funding is needed beyond the normal school operating budget.

Things to Consider

- Teacher training is essential. The Theory of Multiple Intelligences is not the same as learning styles and teachers must have an understanding of how the various intelligences work and are present in each student in order to make the appropriate alterations to curriculum and instruction.

- It is essential that good, accurate baseline data and results are kept.

Current Progress and Results

- In 1997, over 90% of students earned credit for all of their respective courses, and 92% passed the state assessment tests.

School and Demographic Information

Neumann School
2447 W. Granville Avenue
Chicago, IL 60659

- 50 students, grades 6–12; 5 professional staff; 100% African American; poor; urban

Contact

Barry W. Birnbaum
2447 W. Granville Avenue
Chicago, IL 60659
Voice: 773-761-9565
Fax: 773-761-9565
E-mail: birnbaum@mcs.net
Home page: http://www.asd.com:12792

Second Step: A Violence Prevention Curriculum for Middle School and Junior High School

Washington Irving Middle School, Los Angeles, California

This unique violence-prevention program uses a strong, centralized curriculum, extensive parent involvement and training, and well-coordinated classroom efforts to integrate violence prevention lessons into the core curriculum as well as into students' lives outside of school.

The Program's Goals

- ◆ To reduce impulsive and aggressive behavior by teaching children the pro-social skills of empathy, impulse control, problem solving, and anger management.

- ◆ To implement a schoolwide approach to violence prevention.

- ◆ To improve student behavior, teacher-student rapport, and school climate.

How the Program Works

- ◆ There are three levels of the program, one for each of the three grades (6–8).

- ◆ Teachers are trained extensively in the curriculum of the program, meet regularly during the year to discuss problems, share ideas and successes, and coordinate the curriculum over the three-year period. In addition, paraprofessionals, counselors, and administrators attend the training in order to facilitate better communication and motivation for the program as well as use the program's terminology when they deal with students outside of the classroom.

♦ Several classes also participate in an interschool "Peace Institute" process that uses community and school service projects to take the program's lessons beyond the school walls.

♦ The level one lessons in the Second Step program are taught one day a week during the first semester of the sixth grade by two of each team's three teachers. The 20 or so lessons are carefully planned by the two teachers and the social skills portions of the program are incorporated in the team's academic areas. For example, math teachers often integrate student discussions of social problems and instances of violence in graphical displays of data. Language arts teachers regularly incorporate vocabulary from the program in lessons, an especially important aspect of the program because most of the students in the school speak English as a second language. Social studies teachers often incorporate topics such as stereotyping, racial bigotry, and prejudice into history lessons.

♦ Levels two and three are taught in the seventh and eight grades and build on the skills and knowledge gained during students' previous year's lessons. These two levels consist of eight lessons each.

♦ Students' parents are also offered the opportunity to participate in a parenting program designed to offer parents more skills with supervision and control of their children's behavior.

♦ A peer counseling program, managed by the school's counseling center, identifies and trains students to work as peer counselors and mediators in the seventh and eighth grades. Peer counselors help student deal with minor personal problems, conflicts at school, conflicts at home, and conflicts in the neighborhood.

How the Program is Funded and How Much It Costs

♦ Second Step is funded through school improvement funds. The cost per sixth grade teacher (curriculum and training) is about $300, and about $125 per teacher for seventh and eighth grade teachers. Several of the school's teachers train new faculty members in the curriculum.

Things to Consider

- ◆ Training should be extensive and care should be taken to make sure all teachers are trained effectively. New faculty should be trained as soon as possible to insure continuity in lesson delivery and curriculum.

- ◆ Teachers with strong content approaches may have difficulty with some of the more effective strategies that are used in the program; these teachers should be given opportunities for additional training and opportunities to see how the program benefits students' academic achievement.

- ◆ It appears that most teachers take about a year to become fully skillful in program implementation; care should be taken to give all teachers the support needed to become skillful in curriculum delivery.

- ◆ Getting parents involved in the program is extremely important and communication with parents regarding the program is critical.

- ◆ As with many school improvement efforts, maintaining enthusiasm and commitment is difficult. Administrators and school leaders should support the program fully and, if possible, provide additional rewards or recognition to teachers who are teaching the program.

- ◆ Teachers should be provided time and structure to work together to share and identify problems, coordinate efforts across grade levels, and share successes.

Current Progress and Results

- ◆ School climate has improved noticeably; halls and school areas are more calm with less noise and obvious conflict. The number of school suspensions and discipline referrals has decreased dramatically.

- ◆ Students appear to be enthusiastic and excited about the program. They have indicated that they feel empowered to act in socially responsible ways, and often comment that they feel more enjoyment working with teachers to solve problems rather than feeling powerless and intimidated by teachers.

School and Demographic Information

Washington Irving Middle School
3010 Estara Ave.
Los Angeles, CA 90065

- ◆ 1,600+ students, grades 6–8; 75+ teachers; 96% minority, 80%+ lower middle class; urban

Contact

School

Rona Cole
18200 Colchester Way
Northridge, CA 91326
Voice: 818 366-66508
Fax: 818 360-3048

Second Step

Barbara Guzzo
2203 Airport Way South, Suite 500
Seattle, WA 98134-2027
Voice: 800 634-4449
Fax: 206 343-1445

Supporting At-risk Students

Ellicott Mills Middle School, Ellicott City, Maryland

Ellicott Mills Middle School has addressed several problems regarding at-risk students, including the identification of students with special needs or disabling conditions, by implementing a separate team-based process for intervention, assistance, and problem-solving. In addition, the process also identifies school problems of a more systemic or local nature that may also hinder academic achievement, thus combining individual case management processes with classroom and school improvement processes.

The Program's Goals

♦ To assist students who are at risk of school failure due to academic performance or behavioral concerns while fostering improved instructional practices and school improvement.

How the Program Works

♦ Each year, a Student Support Team is developed that consists of persons from the Pupil Services Team, teachers, administrators, and other staff persons. The goal of this team is to assist students who are at risk of failure, identify the ways that school structures and practices can prevent failure, and recommend actions either on an individual or school-community level. The concept of one team with multiple functions helps facilitate the identification and intervention process for students in need of assistance.

♦ A referral to the team may come from teachers, students, or parents. The chairperson of the team coordinates the agenda and assigns case managers if needed, and maintains all records of events, interventions, and results.

♦ The case manager becomes responsible for collecting all of the needed data to make recommendations for interventions, including the student's educational history, test results, work samples, and any other pertinent information, including interviews with the student's teachers or coaches. Parents are contacted by a Pupil Personnel Worker and the school psychologist observes the student in class and interviews teachers and others about the student's behavior and achievement. The process therefore has moved from the more traditional "refer → test → place," to "request for assistance → problem-solve → intervene."

♦ The program parallels the Individuals with Disabilities Education Act (IDEA) but is directed toward students who in all likelihood will not be identified as qualifying for those services, but who are still in danger of school failure.

♦ Once all of the information is collected, the case manager presents the information to the team who works to provide a problem-solving approach to assisting the student. An action plan is written; interventions can be drawn from a variety of selections and ideas that are tailored by the team to meet the student's needs as closely as possible.

♦ Once the intervention has been implemented, the case manager keeps track of its progress, and evaluates the interventions and assistance and reports to the team and the family.

♦ Requests for assistance and the team's recommendation for interventions can also lead to changes or alterations in the school's structures or policies. For example, if there are many requests for assistance to improve homework completion, the team may study the problem more closely as a schoolwide phenomenon rather than intervening for individual students. The goal is to reduce the possibility for student failure, which may mean changing school policies or procedures to eliminate deterrents to school success, but without lowering academic standards.

How the Program is Funded and How Much It Costs

♦ Most of the costs associated with this program are absorbed in the school's normal operating budget. Additional funds from grants or from outside agencies such as Drug-free Schools, violence prevention programs, and so forth can also be used.

Things to Consider

- This is a time-consuming program, and requires common meeting time for personnel involved in the program.

- Facilitation and group management training will be helpful as many of the problems encountered by the team can be emotional, difficult, and complex. Members need good problem-solving and communication skills.

- Case loads can become too large, making it difficult to set priorities for interventions and problems.

Current Progress and Results

- Special education referrals have decreased significantly.

- Faculty and staff have a more holistic view of their students; that is, the team intervention process helps gather information about the students that is often unknown by teachers. Before developing a plan, all barriers to learning are considered, which often leads to additional information about the students.

- The process has resulted in closer monitoring of academic achievement and behavior for referred students. In addition, the intervention evaluation helps identify processes that are effective.

- Support Team members often act as mentors or peer coaches to other teacher staff members as they deal with individual cases.

School and Demographic Information

Ellicott Mills Middle School
4445 Montgomery Road
Ellicott City, MD 21043

- 430 students, grades 6–8; 45 staff; 75% white; varied incomes; suburban

Contact

Eileen Woodbury
10910 Route 108
Ellicott City, MD 21042

Dave Scuccimara
4445 Montgomery Road
Ellicott City, MD 21043
Voice: 410-313-6654
Fax: 410-313-6833
E-mail: www.howard.k12.md.us

World of Work—Mathematics for At-risk Students

Stewart Middle School, Fort Defiance, Virginia

This program is used to help special education students who have difficulty with mathematics experience mathematics as it relates to real-life work and employment. It is unique in the way the project improves students' math skills by involving them in employment situations. Another unique aspect of this program is how students participate in a local partnership with a university to provide support for an event that leads to real-life applications and rewards for parents.

The Program's Goals

◆ To provide hands-on and application opportunities for at-risk students in the area of mathematics.

How the Program Works

◆ For a six-week period, students become "employees" of the school and class. They fill out employment applications; conduct, critique, and experience employment interviews; and, once hired, perform a variety of duties that are linked to mathematics skills. Students are "paid" imaginary money that they deposit in a checking account, which money can be spent for various items provided by the teacher and school. Students are paid or fined based on work attitudes, appropriate dress, punctuality, and other employment expectations.

◆ The jobs the students complete are those that have been designed by the teachers and by other school staff persons. For example, students calculate the amount of paint needed to paint the school's auditorium and how much it will cost, including labor; they calculate the cost to resurface the school's tennis courts, including materials and labor; they calculate all of the costs related to relamping the school's lighting fixtures; and a number of other activities that require knowledge and skills in estimating, averaging, graphing, and problem-solving.

- Employee meetings are held to discuss work progress, problems, and other employment-related items.

- Students are also contracted and employed through a local university to provide announcement materials for a summer conference that takes place on campus. Students use a variety of mathematics and computer applications to design the products. Design, production, distribution, and marketing costs are calculated for the project. Students are "paid" as normal but also receive complimentary registrations for parents to attend the conference.

How the Program is Funded and How Much It Costs

- No additional funding is needed for this program other than transportation to the university for materials distribution.

Things to Consider

- Extensive record keeping is necessary.

- Additional, comprehensive planning and organization are critical, as the students are involved in a variety of activities in different locations and at different times. Additional supervision could be needed to address this problem.

Current Progress and Results

- All participants reported enjoying the six-week class and activities.

- Student grades for this program are higher than at any other time during the year.

- Skills learned in the class generalized into the students' other classes, most notably their vocational classes. Skills also generalized into the students' part-time jobs outside of school.

- Students appeared to have improved their self-esteem and self-concept by experiencing high levels of meaningful success.

- The school received very positive public relations through its partnership involvement, as well as positive responses from parents who benefitted from the students' successes.

School and Demographic Information

S.G. Stewart Middle School
PO Box 37
Fort Defiance, VA 24437

♦ 800 students, grades 6–8; 50 teachers; 90% white; middle class; rural

Contact

Angela Urgo
Rt. 1 Box 179K
Crimora, VA 24431
Voice: 540-363-0809
E-mail: aurgo@pen.k12.va.us
School home page: http://www.augusta.k12.va.us/sms

Programs for Student Learning: How to Think Big with Small Resources

George Washington Carver Middle School, Meridian, Mississippi

Meridian Middle School's unique way of helping students through academic struggles uses both before-school and after-school programs. It is also innovative in the manner in which some of the funds to support the program come from the local housing authority, and how parents are used to support the program.

The Program's Goals

♦ To help with remedial academic progress for at-risk and other students.

♦ To help students catch up, stay caught up, or get ahead in academic work.

How the Program Works

♦ Each middle school academic team has at least one mathematics or language arts teacher who helps students for one hour before school begins each day. Student participation is voluntary, and students can attend if they need extra help, need assistance with homework, want to learn a new skill, and so forth. Students also use this time to work on various research projects and to get access to computers and other technology they need for their work. Students may also use the library, visit the computer laboratories, or eat breakfast during this time.

♦ The after-school program is called "Do Homework First and Then Play" and lasts for two hours after the end of the school day on Mondays, Tuesdays, and Thursdays. The first hour is taken up with homework assistance and completion and the second hour is organized play and games.

How the Program is Funded and How Much It Costs

- The early bird before-school program is funded with Title I funds; teachers are paid an hourly wage comparable to their normal salary.

- The after-school program is funded by the local housing authority, which also arranges for paid parent-assistants to help with the after-school program.

- The school district pays for the additional bus transportation needed for the after-school program.

Things to Consider

- Finding teachers who want to put in the extra hours can be difficult, even though both the before-school and after-school programs require little additional planning; students come with specific needs for help.

- Arranging transportation, both for the morning and after-school programs can be difficult; it helps to be as creative as possible and to emphasize the academic nature of the programs.

- There can be conflicts with other after-school programs and activities such as athletic practices, band or choral practices, and so forth.

- Parent support is critical, and parent support is more likely to be present if the programs are communicated and announced well.

Current Progress and Results

- Over the nearly ten years the before-school program has been in place, grades, test scores, and overall academic achievement has risen steadily. In addition, improved student self-esteem, as measured by discipline referrals, homework completion, and so forth, appears to be much greater each year.

- The after-school program has been in place for only a year and a half, and few results have been measured. However, even without firm academic results, the relationship between the parents who are teaching assistants and the school has improved.

School and Demographic Information

George Washington Carver Middle School
900 44th Avenue
Meridian, MS 39307

♦ 600 students, grades 6–7; 44 teachers; 75% African American, 25% white; 75% free and reduced lunch; urban

Contact

Robert M. Markham
900 44th Avenue
Meridian, MS 39307
Voice: 601-484-4482
Fax: 601-484-4942

Project ALERT

Best Foundation for a Drug Free Tomorrow, Los Angeles, California

This innovative approach to preventing substance abuse among middle school students is a skills-based, motivational curriculum. In addition, it is a long-term program that takes place over a two-year period. Long-term evaluation research indicates that it is one of the best programs of its type in the country.

The Program's Goals

- To prevent teenage nonusers from experimenting with drugs of all types.
- To prevent teenage experimenters from becoming regular users.

How the Program Works

- Project ALERT is facilitated by classroom teachers over a two-year period.
- Eleven lessons form a core for the curriculum and three additional booster lessons are implemented in the second year of the program.
- The program is based on the social influence model, and gives students the motivation, skills, and opportunity to practice resisting those drugs used first and most often by middle school students: alcohol, tobacco, marijuana, and inhalants.
- The program is video-based and makes use of extensive role-playing, student discussions, and small group activities.
- Teachers are trained during a day-long session to use a wide variety of instructional strategies that are directed toward the program's goals.
- Subsequent to the teacher training, teachers receive the entire instructional package of materials at no charge. The included materials contain detailed lesson plans, 2 demonstration videos, 8 student videos, 12 posters, and an optional teen-leader manual.

♦ Once trained, teachers regularly receive updated curriculum materials and videos, a technical assistance newsletter, and additional reenforcement for their efforts at no additional cost. A toll-free telephone number is provided for additional support.

♦ The curriculum counters students' beliefs that "everyone takes drugs" by using statistics and testimony showing that most teenagers don't use drugs, by teaching skills to counter social pressures, and by focusing on resisting internal and external pressures.

♦ The curriculum is divided into five types of lessons, which were designed with the middle school student in mind:

  • Motivating nonuse of drugs;

  • Identifying pressures to use drugs, learning to resist pressures, and practicing resistance skills;

  • Reviewing the key ideas and skills for avoiding drug use;

  • Inhalant abuse and smoking;

  • Reinforcing positive behaviors.

How the Program is Funded and How Much It Costs

♦ The program is subsidized by the BEST Foundation for a Drug Free Tomorrow, a part of the Conrad N. Hilton Foundation, which keeps costs for participants minimal.

♦ The cost for teacher training and materials is minimal; an $85 registration fee is required for the training and all materials are provided.

Things to Consider

♦ To achieve the desired results, the curriculum should be taught as designed and written. Research studies indicate that adherence to the curriculum is critical for success. This does not mean, however, that student experiences, concerns, and ideas are not to be included.

♦ The curriculum, however, is designed in such a way that teachers may include current events about national or local drug-related issues in the curriculum, as well as opportunities for students to become involved in local drug-prevention efforts and projects.

Current Progress and Results

- ◆ Project ALERT is one of the few nationally distributed programs that has met with consistent success. In schools using Project ALERT, there has been:
  - A one-third reduction in marijuana use;
  - A 50% to 60% reduction of heavy smoking among experimenters;
  - A significant reduction in the number of students quitting smoking completely;
  - An initial curbing of alcohol use.

- ◆ The program has been successful in a wide range of socioeconomic and ethnic settings and also has been successful with both low-risk and high-risk students.

- ◆ The program has been given an "A" rating from *Making the Grade: A Guide to School Drug Prevention Programs*.

School and Demographic Information

BEST Foundation for a Drug Free Tomorrow
725 S. Figueroa St.
Los Angeles, CA 90017

Contact

G. Bridget Ryan, Marion Matison, or Teri McHale
725 S. Figueroa St.
Los Angeles, CA 90017
Voice: 800-253-7810
Fax: 213-623-0585

Extracurricular Programs

These programs help students make better use of time, participate in games, sports, and other activities, and continue learning:

Starting an Intramural Program: Macario Garcia Middle (Texas)

> This large middle school's intramural program includes nearly every student in the school and is focused on participation, fun, and cooperation

Intramurals: Everyone's a Winner: Murphysboro Middle (Illinois)

> This intramural program is uniquely linked to the school's advisory program and uses no regular class time, using instead lunch, after-school, and evenings

Promoting Peace in the Classroom: Random Acts of Kindness: Hilltonia Middle (Ohio)

> Based on the national Random Acts of Kindness movement, the school uses a total-school approach that is focused on building positive behaviors and improving academic achievement

Prejudice Reduction Program—Peer Leaders: Geneva Middle (New York)

> Students are used as trainers and peer leaders in the school with coordinated efforts at eliminating prejudices based on cultural or ethnic differences in our diverse society

TOPS—Teachers, Organizations, and Parents for Students: ASPIRA (District of Columbia)

> This program is designed for Hispanic students in middle schools and uses a team approach, good goal-setting, and careful monitoring of student progress

Starting an Intramural Program

Macario Garcia Middle School, Sugarland, Texas

A good intramural program of activities for middle school students is often one of the best ways to promote good citizenship, health, and morale, as well as a great deal of learning. This large middle school's intramural program is innovative and unique because it includes nearly every student in the school and is organized in a fashion that concentrates on participation, fun, learning, and building common bonds across the school.

The Program's Goals

- ◆ To provide opportunities and activities that promote team-building among students.
- ◆ To focus on cooperation and participation instead of competition.

How the Program Works

- ◆ The program is divided into sections based on advisory groups; each grade level has about 15 teachers.
- ◆ Using the advisory groups, the program coordinator and the coordinator's five assistants divide the groups among themselves. Each group participates in a number of "challenges" that are based on typical games, sports, and activities, and on atypical, or "goofy," games and contests.
- ◆ Intramural games take place on Tuesdays (sixth grade), Wednesdays (seventh grade), and Thursdays (eighth grade).
- ◆ Throughout the year, a wide variety of carefully organized, managed, and sequenced games and contests take place. Scores, based on advisory groups, are kept, but the primary focus is on participation as opposed to competing against advisory groups.
- ◆ Students are also recognized for their participation and contribution throughout the year; each individual student is recognized in some fashion at least once a year.

How the Program is Funded and How Much It Costs

♦ The program costs $1,500 to $1,800 per year. Funds come from both the school operating budget and from the school's Parent-Teacher Organization.

Things to Consider

♦ A program as varied and comprehensive as this one needs several facilities and areas in which to hold the games and contests. Indoor as well as outdoor activities and areas are necessary. Large areas are also needed for some events with large numbers of participants.

♦ The program and schedule of events needs to be very well organized and planned for an entire school year.

♦ Supervision is critical; this program uses a coordinator and five other teachers to run the program.

♦ The remaining teachers in the school need to see the value of the program in terms of student morale, citizenship, behavior, and learning. Hold an in-service meeting prior to the school year to inform faculty members about the program and its benefits.

♦ Good organization is imperative. Everything from equipment to materials needs to be obtained and planned well in advance. All supervisors need to be thoroughly informed and trained in terms of the activities prior to implementation. A yearly calendar with a schedule of events is very helpful.

Current Progress and Results

♦ Nearly 99% of all students in the school participate throughout the year.

♦ Nearly a third of all of the students also participate in individual tournaments throughout the year.

♦ Morale in the school is quite high, and the intramural program plays a significant role in keeping the morale high.

School and Demographic Information

Macario Garcia Middle School
18550 Old Richmond Road
Sugarland, TX 77478

- ◆ 1400+ students, grades 6–8; 83 teachers; 86% white; middle class; large suburban

Contact

Gary Crissman
18550 Old Richmond Road
Sugarland, TX 77478
Voice: 281-634-3189
E-mail: 049GC050@fortbend.k12.tx.us
School home page: www.fortbend.k12.tx.us/schools/mcms.htm

Intramurals: Everyone's a Winner

Murphysboro Middle School, Murphysboro, Illinois

This intramural program is unique in the way it connects advisory programs, parent involvement, student interests, and academic interdisciplinary instruction. It also is innovative in the way it schedules its events and activities using no regular class time; instead, it uses lunchtime, after-school, Friday evenings, and advisory periods.

The Program's Goals

- ◆ To include all students in special activities that will increase self-esteem and feelings of worth.

- ◆ To link parent involvement in the school with nonacademic and noncompetitive activities.

- ◆ To link interdisciplinary instructional units with nonacademic activities.

How the Program Works

- ◆ A variety of both sports and nonsports games and activities are planned and scheduled throughout the school year.

- ◆ The events and activities take place during lunch, after school, on Friday evenings, and periodically during certain advisory periods.

- ◆ The evening events are enhanced by the addition of refreshments, board games and other quiet activities, and conversation.

- ◆ Interdisciplinary, thematic units of study include plans for intramural activities that are closely linked to the academic learning goals for the units; the intramural activities take place during the same time frame as the units of study are being implemented in the regular classrooms.

How the Program is Funded and How Much It Costs

◆ Funded locally by the school board, the program's annual costs are comparable to a coaching stipend (about $1,100). The Parent Advisory Group also supplies additional materials such as T-shirts, ribbons, awards, and guest speaker fees.

Things to Consider

◆ All intramural activities require a great deal of supervision and management—someone needs to direct many of the activities and games. Assignment of an individual who can handle large groups of students, as well as keep well-organized, is very important.

Current Progress and Results

◆ Parent involvement in school activities and functions has improved dramatically; 50 to 100 parents regularly attend parent advisory meetings.

◆ Parent attendance at open house events has improved to nearly 85% of all parents.

◆ Return of evaluation surveys from parents rose to over 90%.

◆ Student attendance has improved.

◆ Teacher interest in both the intramural activities and events has increased, and teacher involvement in the program has increased.

◆ The program has resulted in very positive public relations and publicity for the school, as student and parent attendance and involvement improved.

◆ The external school community has become more aware of the school, its culture, and its achievements.

School and Demographic Information

Murphysboro Middle School
2125 Spruce Street
Murphysboro, IL 62966

- ◆ 635 students, grades 6–8; 40+ teachers; 85% white; 50% free/reduced lunch; small/rural

Contact

Sharon H. Johnson
2125 Spruce Street
Murphysboro, IL 62966
Voice: 618-684-3041
Fax: 618-687-1042
E-mail: johnson@intrnet.net

Promoting Peace in the Classroom: Random Acts of Kindness

Hilltonia Middle School, Columbus, Ohio

This unique middle school program is based on the national Random Acts of Kindness movement and uses a total-school approach to build positive, responsible, values, in the student body, which allows the school to focus less on behavior, discipline, and management, and more on academic achievement and school improvement.

The Program's Goals

♦ To create a safe, peaceful environment in school classrooms through kind acts, which allows school staff members to perform their jobs more effectively and to help students reach their full academic potential.

♦ To help students value themselves and the cultural diversity of the school by recognizing acts of kindness.

♦ To encourage students to seek peaceful solutions to situations that cause conflict, stress, and distractions during the school day.

How the Program Works

♦ A local business sponsors the program and provides each school staff person (teachers, custodians, lunchroom personnel, etc.) with a pad of 100 "Kindness Slips" to distribute to students who are caught committing an act of kindness in the school. Besides teachers, others in the school community give kindness slips; for example, custodians give slips to students for reporting various maintenance problems; lunchroom workers give slips for good manners, reporting problems, or taking the time to help keep the lunchroom clean and orderly.

♦ Students caught committing an act of kindness fill out the slip with brief information about the act.

♦ Kindness slips are collected and each week one slip is randomly drawn from each homeroom; this student is designated the "Honoree of the Week" and is given a gift certificate for a free pizza from the sponsor.

♦ Homeroom designee slips are collected from across the school and a "School Kindness Honoree of the Week" is drawn. The student whose slip is drawn is given a custom school T-shirt.

♦ This process forms the focal point for attention to kindness, positive behavior, and other values through other curriculum areas. Teachers often incorporate lessons on resolving conflict and citizenship into their daily teaching; art teachers have students develop personal logos that reflect kind attitudes; physical education teachers incorporate kindness into their lessons as sportsmanship; science teachers use peace and kindness as a theme in lessons on the environment.

How the Program is Funded and How Much It Costs

♦ The program is funded through a community-business partnership with a local pizza company. The local business contributes the pads of slips, individual flyers that are distributed to students, parents, and teachers, and the pizza and T-shirts.

Things to Consider

♦ During the beginning of the program, care should be taken to consistently define throughout the school what constitutes an act of kindness as opposed to normal expectations.

♦ Care should also be taken to ensure that undue attention is not given to consistently disruptive students; that is, there should be representation from across the school student community and the program should not replace well-designed discipline plans or be used to "bribe" unmotivated students.

♦ Sponsorship from a local business must also be carefully sought, as many partnerships wish to focus strictly on academics. It is also important to stress that such a program is based on continued support for several years.

Current Progress and Results

- The school reports many areas of improvement including:
  - Halls and lunchroom are notably quieter, cleaner, and more orderly;
  - Students are much more likely to intervene in conflicts;
  - There is a great deal more cooperation both in classes and in hallways as students are more likely to help each other;
  - Detention and discipline referrals have dropped significantly;
  - The rate of passing state proficiency exams has increased;
  - Teacher morale has improved;
  - There are more students on the honor roll than prior to the program's implementation;
  - Many parents have commented on the differences in the school;
  - As a family-oriented business, the community business is very pleased with its sponsorship.

School and Demographic Information

Hilltonia Middle School
2345 West Mound Street
Columbus, OH 43204

- 720 students, grades 6–8; 60 staff persons; 80% white; 60% free and reduced lunch; urban

Contact

Stacia A. Smith
5523 Township Road 166
West Liberty, OH 43357-9573
Voice: 937-592-4185
E-mail: sasmith@logan.net

Prejudice Reduction Program—Peer Leaders

Geneva Middle School, Geneva, New York

Geneva Middle School's approach to dealing with prejudice and biases is unique for the way the program uses students as the primary communicators and trainers of other students. The program uses students from a wide range of ethnic cultures, as well as a mix of students from different grades, as the students conduct workshops throughout the school district.

The Program's Goals

- To help students understand people.

- To train and help others with prejudice reduction.

- To become student and adult role models for others in our daily lives.

- To lead workshops for fifth and sixth graders throughout the school district and the community.

How the Program Works

- Recognizing that peer pressure and peer relationships are an important part of middle school students' lives, the school selects a number of volunteer students with diverse backgrounds to be trained and to then conduct workshops in the school and school district.

- Selected students attend a one-day training workshop conducted by school personnel and others knowledgeable about racial bias and prejudices. The workshop focuses on prejudice, stereotypes, cultural differences, and how these phenomena affect human behavior and human lives. Some of the areas covered in the workshop are prejudice and biases regarding gender, nationality, religion, ethnicity, racial identity, occupation, dress, sexual orientation, physical disabilities, and socioeconomic differences. Students are also taught the differences between prejudice and discrimination as well as the different ways people can be discriminated against. Through hands-on, active experiences, the students develop the skills and vocabulary needed to conduct workshops and student-to-student training.

◆ Once the training is completed, the students are released from school on a regular basis to conduct workshops for students around the school district; they also provide conflict mediation within the school.

How the Program is Funded and How Much It Costs

◆ Costs for this program are relatively low and are usually paid from discretionary school funds. Costs are incurred for substitute teachers, transportation, and materials.

Things to Consider

◆ Because the peer leaders are often taken out of class, some accommodation should be made for them, as well as support for making up missed classes and topics.

◆ Faculty and administrator support are crucial to success.

Current Progress and Results

◆ Incidents of racial or cultural conflicts have decreased dramatically in both the middle school and the schools that have conducted the workshops. Fifth grade students who have attended the student-led workshops indicate improved knowledge about prejudice, stereotyping, and discrimination, as well as changed attitudes about students who are different from themselves.

◆ The peer leaders have been very successful in dealing with conflict mediation situations where cultural differences play a part in the conflict, leading to a shift in student attitudes about differences.

School and Demographic Information

Geneva Middle School
63 Pulteney Street
Geneva, NY 14456

- ◆ 600+ students, grades 6–8; 60 staff; 80% white; 40+% free and reduced lunch; small urban

Contact

Paige Blazak or Karen Lucas
63 Pulteney Street
Geneva, NY 14456
Voice: 315-781-4139
Fax: 315-781-0694

Kathy Fuchs-Johnson
BOCES
3501 County Rd 20
Stanley, NY 14561
Voice: 716-526-4665

TOPS—Teachers, Organizations, and Parents for Students

ASPIRA Association, Washington, District of Columbia

This program, sponsored by the ASPIRA Association, is directed at addressing the educational needs of Hispanic middle school students. The process uses a team approach, regular meetings and goal-setting, and careful monitoring of student progress.

The Program's Goals

- To increase the motivation of Hispanic students to achieve academically and personally.

- To develop decision-making and goal-setting skills among Hispanic students.

- To increase the involvement of Hispanic parents and foster trust between them and the school's staff.

- To expand the number of adults that support Hispanic students.

- To promote the development of school practices that help bridge the gap between school and family cultures.

How the Program Works

- Hispanic students are the focal point of the program. Once a student is identified for participation in TOPS, a team is formed to support the student. The team is made up of a parent or other family member, the student, and a staff person who is the Academic Coach for the student.

- Teams meet regularly and follow a step-by-step process to help students articulate academic goals, take actions to meet those goals, and monitor progress. The team members also work on ways to help and support each other.

- The student's goals become the basis for a contract that is agreed on by all of the student's team members. Contracts are monitored closely by the team and the student.

- The academic coach provides guidance, support, and academic assistance when needed. The coach has the primary responsibility for monitoring progress toward student goals; in addition to academic support, the coach provides encouragement, instruction, and social support.

- Programs seem to work best with 20–30 students at the school site.

How the Program is Funded and How Much It Costs

- It is possible to operate this program without any additional funds, but for it to be effective some additional funding is needed. Corporate support from ASPIRA is available on a competitive basis to provide a coordinator, community liaison, or parental involvement coordinator; stipends for academic coaches; program materials such as field trips, training, and speakers; as well as the purchase of the implementation kit.

- Other funding is available through other programs such as drug-free schools funds, business and partnership grants, and Chapter I.

Things to Consider

- Strong support and commitment from the school administration is critical.

- Although it is often difficult, the parental involvement aspect of this program that is needed is crucial to its success. Students need to feel the support from both home and school, and the parents need to know that the school is supporting them in their efforts. It is important to be flexible when scheduling meetings with the team to accommodate parents' needs.

- A program coordinator is needed to keep track of the program and guide its implementation. Even if no funds are available for a salary or stipend, this role is necessary.

Current Progress and Results

- ◆ In the four middle schools where this program has been implemented, ongoing evaluations indicate:

  - Improved grades, academic achievement, and participation in class;

  - Improved self-efficacy as determined through surveys;

  - Improved staff-community relations, including stronger relationships between teachers and Hispanic families;

  - Improved student attitudes toward students; students are much more likely to feel that their teachers care about them, their families, and their culture;

  - Improved student commitment toward the school culture, their own academic success, and their outlook on further education.

School and Demographic Information

- ◆ Currently, there are four urban middle schools using the TOPS approach: Cunningham Middle School in Corpus Christi, Texas; Hogg Middle School in Houston, Texas; Tafolla Middle School in San Antonio Texas; and Escuela Intermedia in Sabana Llana, Puerto Rico.

Contact

Oscar Zuniga-Montero
ASPIRA Association
1444 I Street NW #800
Washington, DC 20005
Voice: 202-835-3600 ext. 118
Fax: 202-835-3613
E-mail: aspira@aol.com

Advisory Programs

These four advisory programs have been around long enough to have excellent track records:

Ongoing Development of an Effective Advisory Program: Goochland Middle (Virginia)

> A unique advisory program that meets once a month for an extended period of time and which has received extensive praise and support from the school's community

Growing an Advisory Program: Bernardsville Middle (New Jersey)

> Long-range planning, goal-setting, and regular, consistent evaluation and assessment set this program apart, as well as the way teachers share and rotate lesson plans

Making the Best Advisories: Wallace Middle (Virginia)

> Built-in flexibility and teacher autonomy are central to the way this school has developed a comprehensive and effective advisory program

Teachers' Advisory Program: Aylor Middle (Virginia)

> Schoolwide coordination of advisory curriculum that still leaves time for dealing with individual or school-related student problems

Ongoing Development of an Effective Advisory Program

Goochland Middle School, Goochland, Virginia

The unique feature of Goochland Middle School's advisory is that it meets only once a month for one hour. Unlike many other advisory programs, this program has been very successful and has received praise from the school community.

The Program's Goals

♦ To implement an advisory program that is focused on students' intellectual, physical, emotional, social, and ethical development.

♦ To provide teachers with the tools and motivation to work toward a successful program.

♦ To provide structured activities and a curriculum within which students and teachers build positive feelings about the school.

How the Program Works

♦ All faculty members are provided in-service training and education about the importance of good advisories, how good advisories work, and how to plan and implement advisory activities.

♦ A committee of faculty members is selected to plan, manage, and communicate the program to the faculty.

♦ All faculty members are assigned a small group of 12 to 15 students.

♦ A 60-minute period is built into the schedule each month to provide time to implement a "class" or set of activities directed toward a specific topic. The topics are identified by the staff and faculty, and activities and plans are developed prior to each month. These topics are then referred to and focused on over the course of the month in regular classes.

♦ These topics are used during the advisories over the eight-month school year:

- Peer relations;
- Teamwork;
- Problem solving;
- Decision making;
- Study skills;
- Career education;
- Drug education;
- Academic performance.

How the Program is Funded and How Much It Costs

♦ No additional funds are used for this program.

Things to Consider

♦ These elements of the program are critical to its success:

- Supportive administrators;
- Dedicated advisory planning committee that meets regularly;
- A wide variety of student activities that are fully planned;
- Effective in service for faculty;
- Student-centered topics that are relevant to students to insure student involvement;
- Open and continual communication among faculty members;
- A yearly evaluation of the program.

Current Progress and Results

♦ The yearly evaluation of the program indicates that students and teachers are highly supportive of the program, its goals, and how it is implemented. The amount of time needed for planning and development by advisory teachers is considerably less than in programs that meet weekly or daily.

School and Demographic Information

Goochland Middle School
2748 Dogtown Road
Goochland, VA 23063

♦ 440 students, grades 6–8; 35 teachers; 66% white, 33% African American, 1% Hispanic; middle class; urban

Contact

Barbara B. Henson
2748 Dogtown Road
Goochland, VA 23063
Voice: 804-556-5387
Fax: 804-556-6269

Growing an Advisory Program

Bernardsville Middle School, Bernardsville, New Jersey

The unique and innovative way this middle school developed its advisory program stands apart from most programs. Its advisory program is based on a comprehensive, long-range plan that is regularly and comprehensively assessed in order to make needed changes. It is also unique in the way teams of teachers share and rotate lesson planning roles.

The Program's Goals

♦ To ensure that each student has a convenient, established relationship with at least one teacher/mentor in the school building.

♦ To assist students in their orientation and adjustment to the middle school setting.

♦ To help students develop appropriate decision-making and problem-solving skills and set goals that will facilitate positive school experiences.

♦ To help students develop a positive self-concept and build peer-group relationships.

♦ To use the small group setting of an advisory to initiate schoolwide practices.

How the Program Works

♦ In 1993, the school established a team-based thematic model for an advisory which was used for the next two years.

♦ In 1995, planning began for a new advisory program that was piloted in 1996 and revised as follows in 1997.

♦ A committee of school faculty members was established to develop a plan of action for implementing an advisory program in the school. This committee developed a program rationale and set goals that were then agreed on by the remaining faculty.

♦ Advisory groups of 12 to 14 students are formed in either a fifth/ sixth grade configuration or a seventh/eighth grade configuration. Each of these groups is then linked to another group to form a "familylike" arrangement. That is, each advisory group contains students from all four grade-levels.

♦ The schedule was altered to accommodate advisory group meetings 3 times a week (in place of homeroom) for 10 minutes, and the groups meet twice a month for 30 minutes each.

♦ Regular monthly faculty meetings are held for program updates, planning, and problem solving. A schoolwide topic is chosen at each faculty meeting; the previous topic and lessons are also evaluated during the monthly meeting.

♦ At the end of the year, the program is fully evaluated by both students and faculty members.

How the Program is Funded and How Much It Costs

♦ A minimal summer stipend is given for the yearly planning committee chairperson. Any other expenses are generally covered through the home-school association.

Things to Consider

♦ With respect to planning and implementing such a program, it is important to carefully consider teachers' contract obligations regarding duties, compensation, and time.

♦ It is important to work through any faculty philosophic differences and try to get as close to consensus as possible. The use of monthly updates and planning at regular faculty meetings allow for generous input from all faculty members.

♦ Planning time is crucial for the success of this type of program; be sure to allow the planning teams to have the necessary time to plan advisory curriculum that is consistent with school needs, the chosen topic, and school goals.

♦ It is important to carefully review and communicate the program's goals, processes, and objectives to students. Students need to know the program's purposes and to be assured that cross-grade-level groups and teacher assignments will be made fairly and equitably.

Current Progress and Results

- Faculty members have become more convinced of the program's effectiveness and appropriateness.

- Faculty members consistently indicate that they enjoy how the program allows them to communicate and work with teachers across grade levels.

- Faculty and students indicate and demonstrate improved school spirit and participation in school activities.

School and Demographic Information

Bernardsville Middle School
141 Seney Drive
Bernardsville, NJ 07924

- 360 students, grades 5–8; 40 teachers; 90% white; suburban

Contact

Dr. Robert Pollack, Kathy Hughes, or Bev Webb
Bernardsville Middle School
141 Seney Drive
Bernardsville, NJ 07924
Voice: 908-204-1816
Fax: 908-953-2184

Making the Best Advisories

Wallace Middle School, Bristol, Virginia

The flexibility and the extensive planning that take place for this advisory program makes the program unique and successful. Advisories often struggle with a variety of issues, but teacher involvement seems to be a continual concern in many schools. At Wallace, the program was designed, planned, and implemented by the entire staff, and the program's built-in flexibility keeps the teacher commitment to the program very high.

The Program's Goals

- ◆ To enhance middle level educators' understanding of the importance of a well-supported advisory program.

- ◆ To ensure that each child in the school has a knowledgeable and supportive adult to whom the child can turn.

- ◆ To generate acceptance of personal responsibility through the advisory program and simultaneously model personal responsibility.

- ◆ To place the advisory program at the center of the educational foundation for the school.

- ◆ To use advisories to enhance and support other aspects of school life and goals.

How the Program Works

- ◆ Students are grouped into small advisory groups of 14 to 16 children. These students are assigned to a school staff member. Nearly all professional staff members have an advisory group.

- ◆ The advisories meet at the beginning of every school day for 25 minutes.

- ◆ Care was taken in the planning of the program to avoid becoming a "catch-all" period that can deteriorate into nonfunctioning groups. The teachers are given a variety of options from which to plan advisory activities, including those that are designed to improve student-teacher relationships.

♦ Included in the program are activities such as:

- Orientation to the next grade level;

- Attention to social problems and issues that arise in the culture;

- Group discussions (and training students to engage productively in discussions) regarding issues relevant to the students;

- Free reading ("Drop Everything and Read");

- Career exploration and guest speakers;

- Closed circuit television programs related to national disasters that are the focus of service learning activities;

- Planning and managing clubs, and/or intramural sports and games;

- Story telling and reading to students.

This list is far from complete. Teachers and teams are encouraged to address issues and develop programs in a manner that best fits their particular students' needs and development.

♦ A great deal of attention is also paid to common misperceptions about advisories. Staff development for the teachers addresses many of the issues that often become problematic for schools. For example, teachers are intentionally told that they are not counselors and that teachers do not have to change their behaviors or become less of an authority than in normal classes.

How the Program is Funded and How Much It Costs

♦ Few additional funds are needed. Some teachers order inexpensive but they avoid buying expensive published "canned" programs.

Things to Consider

♦ It is important to address the concerns of staff members who may be skeptical by continually noting the successes of the program.

♦ It is equally important to work at preventing apathy as programs and activities become too routine.

♦ Some additional funding may be needed.

♦ Planning time is critical. It is important that the schoolwide plans be developed by involving as many staff members as possible. Providing the planning time may be difficult, but it is very important.

♦ Administrative support from both the building administrators and the central office administrators is very important.

♦ Be sure all parents are informed of the program and understand its goals. Parents should be given information about successes and other matters in as many ways as possible.

Current Progress and Results

♦ Discipline has improved schoolwide.

♦ The service-learning projects that have come about as a result of advisory attention have often been instrumental in changing the behavior of certain problem students.

School and Demographic Information

Wallace Middle School
13077 Wallace Pike
Bristol, VA 24202

♦ 430 students, grades 6–8; 38 teachers; 100% white; low to middle income; small town

Contact

Alan Bevins
13077 Wallace Pike
Bristol, VA 24202
Voice: 540-645-2370
Fax: 5540-645-2365
E-mail: dab@naxs.com
Home page: www.wcs.k12.va.us/schools/midd/wms/default.htm

Teachers' Advisory Program

Aylor Middle School, Stephens City, Virginia

What makes this advisory program unique and innovative is the manner in which the curriculum and instruction for the advisory program is coordinated on a schoolwide basis that still leaves opportunities for individual teachers to respond to student issues and problems. Nationally, few advisory programs appear to be effective, and most are very difficult to implement. This program, however, by being centrally managed and coordinated, is well implemented and maintained.

The Program's Goals

- ◆ To help students develop and maintain a positive self-image.

- ◆ To help students respond and develop both socially and emotionally in a positive manner.

- ◆ To give support and guidance for character development.

- ◆ To build community and a sense of belonging for students and staff.

- ◆ To build good student community citizenship.

How the Program Works

- ◆ The advisory program meets daily for 20 minutes; each teacher has an advisory group.

- ◆ The advisory week is divided into coordinated activities that are consistent over the school:

  - • On Monday, each grade level is engaged in different teacher-led activities from sources gathered and agreed on by the faculty. Each grade level focuses on topics that are linked in such a way that students will not experience repeated lessons throughout their three-year enrollment. In the sixth grade, the focus is broad-based and directed toward issues relevant to new middle school students; in the seventh grade, the focus is on relationships; in the eighth grade, the focus is on making good decisions.

- On Tuesdays, additional supportive activities linked to the Monday lesson are used in each advisory room.

- On Wednesdays and Thursdays, topical videos on different but relevant topics are broadcast from the school's library; these short (15 minutes) videos often form a central discussion focus for teachers and students to use throughout the remainder of the week and throughout the regular school day. Longer videos are divided into several short showings.

- On Fridays the entire school engages in "DEAR," a "Drop Everything and Read" period.

♦ The program is very well coordinated and managed, making it "low maintenance" for teachers. This element of the program overcomes one of the most common problems faced by middle school advisory programs, the additional time and work involved for classroom teachers.

How the Program is Funded and How Much It Costs

♦ There are few costs involved in this program, with the exception of a few teacher texts, duplicating expenses, and small rental fees for the videos.

Things to Consider

♦ Great care and consideration should be given to the topics, especially those introduced during the Monday sessions. Some students are reluctant to participate given the nature of some of the topics.

♦ Although this program overcomes many of the objections teachers have regarding advisory programs (planning, effort, times, etc.), it is not uncommon for a few teachers to remain resistant. Care should be taken to ensure that as much central coordination takes place as possible, which will offset some of these objections. In addition, care must be taken to allow for the entire staff's involvement in the initial planning and implementation of the program, and to have significant and meaningful input into the process and into the topics to be studied in each grade level.

♦ Care should be taken in the selection of the videos shown across the school; preliminary viewing of the videos is critical, so time should be allowed for prescreening.

Current Progress and Results

♦ The school enjoys exceptional support for the program from students, teachers, and parents.

♦ Since the program began, inappropriate student behavior has decreased.

♦ The use of the topical videos continues to be a motivating factor in the success of the program, and has resulted in schoolwide awareness of issues and improved morale.

♦ The "DEAR" program, combined with other efforts, has resulted in a significant increase in numbers of books being checked out of the library, as well as in improved reading scores.

School and Demographic Information

Robert E. Aylor Middle School
901 Aylor Road
Stephens City, VA 22655

♦ 760+ students, grades 6–8; 73 teachers; 94% white; primarily middle class; suburban

Contact

Allen Long, Advisory Coordinator, or Larry Mullin, Principal
901 Aylor Road
Stephens City, VA 22655
Voice: 540-869-3736
Fax: 540-869-3704

4

Parents, Partners, and the School Community

There is no doubt that parental involvement in schooling begins to diminish during the middle level years, especially if there are younger siblings at home. There is also evidence that teachers' efforts at getting parents involved in school are weaker and less focused on the whole child than is often the case in elementary school. Chapter 1 discussed some of the unique and creative ways that students and parents are oriented to the middle schools; it is equally important for all schools to demonstrate a strong commitment and ongoing effort at keeping parents actively and meaningfully involved in middle-level education. The key to having meaningful involvement is the extent to which parents are involved in governance, supervision, curriculum development, and volunteering; that is, parental efforts should go far beyond the traditional "we need a chaperone" or cutting out letters activities.

In addition, many schools, businesses, and agencies are seeing how strong partnerships can benefit everyone. Again, the key is the extent to which the involvement of outside agencies and businesses is meaningful involvement; outside agencies and businesses must actively engage in school life, and schools must embrace this engagement and look beyond fund-raising efforts.

Finally, it is important for the schools, especially middle schools, to become once more a central part of their surrounding communities. That is, schools must contribute to the community as the community contributes to them. This chapter has several examples of unique and powerful ways that parents, industries, and communities have brought new meaning to the idea of community and commitment.

Parents

These programs exemplify how parents can be involved in governance, supervision, curriculum development, and volunteering:

TRAC: Building Community Through Volunteerism (A Parent Supervision Model): Lake Oswego Middle (Oregon)

> This program that goes beyond the more traditional ways parent volunteers are used in schools, toward assistance in the form of student supervision

The Transparent School Model: Peabody College (Tennessee)

> This is a technology-driven model for communicating with parents of middle school students that responds to parent needs regardless of school size or complexity

Parent Involvement and Positive Climate—Improved Student Success: Eastwood Middle (Ohio)

> This program uses multiple ways to communicate with parents as well as multiple ways to recognize student achievement and accomplishments

PEP: Parent Empowerment Program: Sarah Scott Middle (Indiana)

> Parents are actively involved in this urban school in many ways as teachers reach out to the community for communication and support

TRAC: Building Community Through Volunteerism (A Parent Supervision Model)

Lake Oswego Junior High School, Lake Oswego, Oregon

This parent-volunteer program is innovative in the way the volunteers become involved in many different facets of school life and assist teachers and principals with the never-ending task of supervising students. Parent involvement in school affairs is one of several factors with a strong influence on student success.

The Program's Goals

◆ To increase adult presence in the school.

◆ To increase adult awareness of school programs, the school environment, and the daily life of the school.

◆ To provide adult supervision support for many activities in the school.

How the Program Works

◆ Parents and other adults volunteer to supervise different activities for certain periods of the school day.

◆ Extensive training is provided several times during the school year for the adults. The focus of the training is on support and presence and the developmental characteristics of middle level children, not discipline or behavior management.

◆ Volunteers work varying amounts of time throughout the school day, depending on their personal and professional schedules.

◆ Parents and other adults have a presence in such activities as:

  • Welcoming students to school in the morning;

- Watching children during the various short "breaks" given students during the day;
- Wandering the school halls as "walkabouts," especially during class changes;
- Supervising and assisting in the computer laboratory;
- Joining in a lunchtime basketball game;
- Monitoring quiet study halls during the lunch hour;
- Monitoring and helping in the cafeteria food line.

♦ Parents are assigned specific roles and duties and a schedule is provided.

How the Program is Funded and How Much It Costs

♦ There are few costs beyond the time and energy involved in managing the program. Suggested cost items are brochures and walkie-talkies.

Things to Consider

♦ Communication and training are critical to the success of such a program; that is, each volunteer should be fully aware of his or her role, specific duties, and expectations.

♦ Emphasis should be placed on the "adult presence" aspect of the program; parents are not there as disciplinarians, but to provide additional adult presence in school activities and areas. Behavior problems should be handled by teachers and administrators.

♦ A cadre of substitute volunteers is also needed to provide for ongoing presence if a parent or other adult cannot be at the school.

♦ A carefully developed schedule and calendar of dates, times, and roles, should be prepared well in advance and distributed to all volunteers. The calendar should be distributed early enough to allow volunteers to rearrange their personal schedules well in advance of their respective volunteer dates (perhaps a month in advance or once each trimester or semester.)

Current Progress and Results

- ◆ There has been a significant decline in student-to-student harassment or teasing during unstructured times (lunch, class changes, passing times, etc.)

- ◆ Incidents of smoking or other inappropriate behaviors in the restrooms has been nearly eliminated.

- ◆ Incidents of physical altercations have diminished to near zero since the inception of this program.

- ◆ Parents have indicated a new and improved appreciation for awareness of the role of the school, the problems facing teachers and administrators, and the developmental characteristics of middle-level children.

- ◆ Parents also indicate a significant increase in their confidence in the school and its staff.

- ◆ Teachers and other school staff have indicated improved student behavior and student and teacher morale throughout the school.

School and Demographic Information

Lake Oswego Junior High School
2500 Country Club Road
Lake Oswego, OR 97034

- ◆ 650 students, grades 7–8; 36 teachers; 94% white; middle- and upper-class; suburban

Contact

Janet Burgess
Lake Oswego Junior High School
2500 Country Club Road
Lake Oswego, OR 97034
Voice: 503-635-0335
Fax: 503-635-0341
E-mail: burgessj@loswego.k12.or.us

The Transparent
School Model

Peabody College,
Vanderbilt University,
Nashville, Tennessee

This technology-driven model for communicating with parents and others in middle schools is an excellent way to respond to parental needs, diversity, and information dissemination regardless of school size or demographics.

The Program's Goals

- ◆ To use voice messaging technology to expand and improve parent involvement and school/home communication.

How the Program Works

- ◆ The Transparent School Model is the name of a particular voice-messaging technology ("voice mail") that is installed in the school.

- ◆ Each teacher in the school has a mailbox within which the teacher can record a daily message that describes what was taught and how it was taught, any homework or assignments that were given, including any unique directions or clarifications that might be needed, and suggestions for ways parents can help with this or any other lesson or topic. For language-minority students and parents, English as a Second Language teachers, volunteers, or other foreign language teachers can help teachers by translating teacher messages into other languages.

- ◆ Parents can call a single number and listen to the daily message.

- ◆ The system also allows for the school or individual teachers to use the "outcall" feature for attendance or absence information, emergency notifications, or for individual student recognition or congratulations for outstanding performances.

How the Program is Funded and How Much It Costs

- The technology to support the Transparent School Model is typically purchased by individual schools; costs vary from $10,000 to $15,000 per installation. Ongoing costs involve the monthly telephone line charges.

- Many schools are using business partnerships to assist in the funding of this project, especially schools in which large number of employees' children are enrolled. Title I and Goals 2000 funds may also be used for this technology.

Things to Consider

- As with any innovative program, the success of this model depends heavily on careful introduction of the model and technology to parents and teachers.

- Careful and thorough planning for the implementation is crucial.

- Thorough, ongoing staff development for teachers must take place throughout the project; new faculty training is a must.

- Marketing and explaining the system to parents takes time and commitment on the part of many individuals in the school.

- The model works best when it is used as an integrated means for routine school-to-home communication, and by using it as a means to build outside partnerships.

- A telephone in every classroom is not absolutely necessary, but helpful.

- Using the system takes classroom teachers approximately five minutes per day.

Current Progress and Results

- Over 2,000 schools in the United States are currently using this or another form of voice messaging to improve parent communication.

- In locations where implementation has been taken very seriously and there is staff commitment to the project, at least half of the school population's parents call daily for information. In addition, homework completion rates rise dramatically, grades are improved, and student failures decrease.

♦ There have been correlation studies completed that suggest scores on standardized tests and grade point averages improve when this system is used properly.

Contact

Jerold P. Bauch, Director
Box 81
Peabody College
Nashville, TN 37203
Voice: 615-322-8080
Fax: 615-343-5670
E-mail: bauchjp@ctrvax.vanderbilt.edu

Parent Involvement and Positive Climate— Improved Student Success

Eastwood Middle School, Pemberville, Ohio

Consistent, ongoing, comprehensive, and positive communication is what makes Eastwood's parent involvement program different and unique. The school uses a variety of student incentives, recognitions, and rewards to maintain and improve the school's climate. The community is publicly invited into the school.

The Program's Goals

- To promote and develop parent involvement as an important factor in positive school climate.
- To demonstrate the effects of positive school climate on improved student achievement and success.

How the Program Works

- The leadership team of the school, along with the parent organization, plan a complete school year's calendar of events that includes orientations, open houses, breakfasts and teas, conferences, dances and parties, and other regular events. In addition, the team plans for the awards and recognition events in which parents play significant roles as facilitators and presenters.
- Parent involvement is also organized and implemented through homework hotlines, homework check systems, a parent section in the school library, and programs to help parents deal with pre-adolescent students and the challenges middle school students face daily.
- Communications to parents and the community are regular and on-going and include not only student achievement and success, but faculty and staff accomplishments.

- The school climate program is tied closely to the parent involvement program and includes recognition of students of the week, month, and year, as well as recognitions for superior citizenship, birthdays, academic projects, and community involvement and participation. Academic success is emphasized heavily. In addition to the traditional "honor roll," the school rewards all students for maintaining or improving academic progress. Rewards are given by faculty members throughout the year. These rewards can be used to "bid" on products and items at the end of the year. These items are purchased through the student council and the principal's office.

- Each reward and recognition program is constantly evaluated as to its effectiveness and whether or not it is supporting student achievement and improved academic performance.

How the Program is Funded and How Much It Costs

- Costs vary and depend largely on the extent to which the school purchases items for rewards and recognitions, and how elaborately designed the parent involvement program is. However, most costs can be covered through small business grants, donations, and normal funding processes.

Things to Consider

- Involving everyone is essential; this means all areas of the community as well as all areas of the school. A sense of ownership is crucial; therefore, planning and implementation should involve as many persons as possible.

- Communications and outreach into the community and to parents should be ongoing and include more than just recognitions. Newsletters should include items about the school's philosophy, academic results, opportunities for involvement, and items about homework policies and procedures. Communication should be two-way; communication from parents and the community should not be hindered or discouraged in any way.

Current Progress and Results

- School climate has never been better, which has resulted in fewer discipline problems, higher academic achievement, and greater school pride and commitment.

- Parents are involved in every aspect of the school, including governance and policy development.

School and Demographic Information

Eastwood Middle School
4800 Sugar Ridge Road
Pemberville, OH 43450

- 450 students, grades 6–8; 44 teachers; 98% white; rural farming community

Contact

Susan L. Wynn
3329 State Route 281
Wayne, OH 43466

Linda Caughey
1738 Kahler Road
Pemberville, OH 43450
Voice: 419-288-2851
Fax: 419-288-2851

Parent Empowerment Program (PEP)

Sarah Scott Middle School, Terre Haute, Indiana

Sarah Scott's parent program is unique in several ways, but the most innovative ways it is being implemented are the way in which the school reaches out to the urban community for support; the way that faculty teams demonstrate the reciprocal nature of the relationship by making home visits; and the way that parents are used meaningfully and effectively in all aspects of school life.

The Program's Goals

♦ To help break the familial cycle of failure, apathy, poverty, and abuse by working with families along with their children.

♦ To engage parents in joining with school personnel to identify and overcome barriers that prevent parents from being more involved in the education of their children.

♦ To provide meaningful and varied means for parents to become involved in the life of the school.

How the Program Works

♦ As part of a larger partnership effort, the school recognized the need for strong partnerships between the school and its parents. Research suggests that parental involvement in schools is one determinant of higher achievement for students. A grant-supported parent coordinator manages, organizes, and directs many of these efforts.

♦ School officials, teachers, and other school community members hold recruiting meetings in the community—in churches, housing offices, elementary schools, homes, community centers, and any other area where parent contacts and meetings can be held. These outreach meetings contribute to making parents feel less threatened by the school, and help parents feel more comfortable in their own environments. In addition, teachers and faculty teams make home visits for the purpose of recognizing positive behavior and success as well as problems.

♦ Parents volunteer for and are placed on one of ten subcommittees that reach into all areas of school life including discipline, curriculum, communication, and climate. In addition, each subcommittee includes at least one member of each teaching team, creating a circular communication system. Great effort is made to keep a constant flow of communication moving throughout the groups.

♦ Much effort is also made to assure that parents are always comfortable in the school. A room has been set aside in the 80-year-old building for parents to work in and support the school.

♦ The empowered parents and school staff support, organize, and sponsor a number of different community programs, including:

- Parenting and social skills development;
- Voter registration drives;
- Parent-to-parent mentoring;
- Transportation and child care for attendees of school and community functions;
- Parent security teams;
- Families in support of educational equity;
- Saturday school functions;
- Speakers, tutoring, field trip coordination and chaperoning;
- Fund-raising;
- Facility improvement;
- Morning, after-school, and evening events such as parent breakfasts, open houses, school pride nights, school orientations, and career days;
- Parents also have a sophisticated telephone network to inform other parents of upcoming events and important school functions.

♦ The Parent Advisory Council consists of a parent leader and representatives from all other subgroups including volunteer groups. This group operates within school guidelines and authority, but in a fairly autonomous manner, as it has become a part of the school leadership and governance.

How the Program is Funded and How Much It Costs

- ◆ Original funding came from a $65,000 grant from an educational foundation. Funds were originally used for staff development, furnishing the parent room, purchasing supplies and materials, subscribing to a number of periodicals for use by parents and staff, and visits to other schools to see exemplary programs.

- ◆ The parent coordinator is funded through a Drug-Free Schools grant, and other parts of the program are funded as collaborative projects with local human service agencies, other institutions, and community buildings. The effectiveness, successes, and visibility of the program has been instrumental in helping the school raise funds for the programs.

Things to Consider

- ◆ Startup funds are essential, but once the program is going and is successful, few funds are needed to maintain the program.

- ◆ Changes in attitude come slowly; do not expect things to change for the better overnight.

- ◆ All persons involved need training and staff development, including parents. Skills development, particularly leadership skills, do not come easily for many parents, especially those who have had little school success.

- ◆ Cooperative planning with interested community stakeholders will help provide momentum and energy for the project and lead to better implementation.

- ◆ Early identification of strong, charismatic parent leaders will help much of the early recruitment efforts. Pay little attention to socioeconomic status or educational attainment. It is very important to maintain a diverse group that is reflective of the community and respectful of cultural differences.

- ◆ It is helpful if the school administrator is a recognized community leader and has contacts and a network within the community.

◆ No two parent-empowerment programs will be exactly alike; it is important that the program be customized to the individual school's community, needs, students, and parents.

◆ Be assured that fear and discomfort will be present for many, and this is to be expected and welcomed.

Current Progress and Results

◆ In addition to numerous national awards and recognitions for its parent program, the school has been featured in over 30 national publications.

◆ The secretary of education and other dignitaries have visited the school.

◆ Parent attendance at school functions has increased tenfold, and the number of parent-sponsored and generated activities has soared.

School and Demographic Information

Sarah Scott Middle School
2000 South 9th Street
Terre Haute, IN 47802

◆ 400+ students, grades 6–8; 36 teachers; 20% minority; 60+% free or reduced cost lunches; urban

Contact

Dr. Sandra K. Kelley
2000 South 9th Street
Terre Haute, IN 47802
Voice: 812-462-4381
Fax: 812-462-4370
E-mail: skk2@galileo.vigoco.k12.in.us
Home page: http://www.vigoco.k12.in.us/users/scotms/index/html

Partners

These two programs demonstrate how schools can enrich curriculum by establishing a partnerships with outside agencies and businesses:

The New York Academy of Medicine Junior Fellows Program: New York City Middle Schools (New York)

> Extracurricular program that brings medical professionals and middle school students together for research, mentoring, and prevocational activities

Scientists/Engineers in the Classroom: Trent Lott Middle (Mississippi)

> Working scientists and engineers visit the school and teach a variety of science lessons that are based on real-world problems; students take a trip to scientists' workplace

The New York Academy of Medicine Junior Fellows Program

New York City Middle Schools, New York, New York

This cross- and extracurricular activity brings middle school students and medical professionals together for research, mentoring, and prevocational activities. Although implemented in the New York City area, the format for this program could be used in any location.

The Program's Goals

- ◆ To help middle school students develop health and life-management skills.

- ◆ To increase students' knowledge of current health, medical, and ethical issues.

- ◆ To inspire and motivate students to be critical thinkers.

- ◆ To interest middle school students in science, medicine, and research, and to make them aware of these fields as career possibilities.

- ◆ To teach students how to access information electronically and to help them develop good library and research skills.

How the Program Works

- ◆ There are four main components of the program:
  - A comprehensive health education program for middle school students;
  - Telecommunications, Internet, and library information skills;
  - Interaction with practicing health professionals;
  - Introduction to medical and scientific ethics.

- ◆ The program lasts 11 weeks; 25 middle school students are chosen to participate in the program.

♦ Students are paired with mentor physicians who help them choose a particular research question.

♦ Tours of the medical center and hospital are taken by the students, and they attend seminars and workshops about medical fields, careers, and other topics chosen by the students. Hospital staff, mentor physicians, and other health educators present the workshops and seminars.

♦ Science teachers, medical library staff members, and other health professionals teach the students to perform medical research investigations using the Internet and other medical databases. In addition, students are taught how to evaluate and assess the worth and value of various pieces of research.

♦ Students use these findings to write a comprehensive research paper on their respective topics and then present their findings as part of a formal program graduation ceremony.

How the Program is Funded and How Much It Costs

♦ Funding needs are minimal, but include transportation and other educational supplies. Most support comes from volunteers from both the school districts and the medical centers.

Things to Consider

♦ Preplanning and public relations are critical to this program's success.

♦ Medical centers and hospitals benefit considerably from this and other similar programs, as the program offers young physicians and other medical professionals the opportunity to perform community service, which is often required by employers. It also provides medical centers with an opportunity for positive public relations and image-building in an era when the vast majority of publicity about medicine and healthcare is negative.

♦ Access to the Internet and a good medical library are critical for the students to be able to perform comprehensive research.

♦ Support from the participating schools' teachers and administrators is also critical for maintenance of the program.

Current Progress and Results

- The New York City program is in its third year, and is expanding to include two additional middle schools.

- A formal evaluation of this program was conducted in the fall of 1996. The findings from the evaluation suggest that:

  - Students, parents, teachers, librarians, and other participants felt the program very worthwhile;

  - The research and writing skills of over three-fourths of the students improved;

  - Half of the students leave the program with a strong interest in careers in health fields;

  - All of the students indicated positive feelings about their mentors.

- One student created a children's cartoon book to illustrate a particular disease. The medical center was so impressed with the student's work that she was offered a summer internship to help develop educational materials for young patients.

School and Demographic Information

This program has been implemented in seven urban middle schools, all having different socioeconomic levels. The approximate ethnic makeup of the schools is African American 30%, Hispanic 30%, Asian American 30%, white 10%.

Contact

Leslie Goldman
Office of School Health Programs
New York Academy of Medicine
1216 Fifth Avenue
New York, NY 10029

Scientists/Engineers in the Classroom

Trent Lott Middle School, Pascagoula, Mississippi

Schools have been using "gee-whiz" science activities and speakers to make science exciting for students for a number of years. This middle school, however, takes the concept to a new, unique, and innovative level. Working scientists and engineers visit the school on a regular basis and teach science lessons that are based on real-world problems and applications. Students then take a trip to visit the scientist's workplace.

The Program's Goals

♦ To promote the scientific literacy and science career awareness of middle school students.

♦ To demonstrate how practicing professional teachers and practicing business/industry science professionals can collaborate to develop innovative, thoughtful, and relevant science lessons.

♦ To help students make connections with the world beyond the classroom and home.

How the Program Works

♦ For a period of six weeks and for one day each week for about an hour, a scientist or an engineer teaches a science lesson to seventh and eighth grade students.

♦ The regular teacher remains in the room and assists the guest teacher with the lesson. A variety of lesson types are used, including demonstrations, videos, presentations, and games.

♦ Each six-week visiting scientist or engineer focuses on one area of an industry-specific discipline; for example, the chemist facilitates the solving of a chemistry problem, the design engineer focuses on designing a product to solve a problem, and so forth.

♦ The format followed during the seven-week period is:

- Week 1: Introduction: Who we are and what we do;

- Week 2: Science problem-solving within the industry;

- Week 3: Student activities: Solving problems as scientists/engineers do it;

- Week 4: Students as practicing scientists/engineers;

- Week 5: Communicating results (of student investigations);

- Week 6: Tour of the workplace;

- Week 7: Careers in this industry as scientists and engineers; evaluation.

- Each of these teaching modules is written out, evaluated, and developed into a thematic unit that others might use.

How the Program is Funded and How Much It Costs

- Little additional funds are needed. Laboratory and science supplies are available at the school through regular funding procedures and most of the materials used by the visiting professional are supplied by their respective firms.

- For the field trip to the workplace, the school provides transportation as well as a substitute for the teacher to accompany the students.

Things to Consider

- Ideally, the program works best when a team of teachers and industry professionals meet and plan the scope and sequence of events prior to the school year. Time should be taken to plan and develop the schedule as early as possible, to accommodate industry professionals' time and work constraints.

- It is sometimes difficult to find industry professionals who have the flexibility needed to commit to a six-week period of school visits and lessons; however, by networking through the industry, a cadre of professionals who are eager to help can be found.

- Any additional funds for purchases and materials should be requested early.

- Any legal agreements or liability arrangements between the school and an outside firm should be investigated and completed thoroughly prior to implementing the program.

Current Progress and Results

- The program has been in place for over five years and has now been implemented at a number of other middle schools and school districts.

- The program has been presented at a number of industry-specific conferences and meetings as a model for collaboration and community involvement.

- Students indicate a much stronger preference for science and science-related topics.

- Overall, student and teacher evaluations regarding the program have been positive.

- A more formal evaluation and assessment of the program are under way.

School and Demographic Information

Trent Lott Middle School
2234 Pascagoula St.
Pascagoula, MS 39567

- 510+ students; grades 6–8; 43 teachers and staff; 73% white; a wide range of socioeconomic backgrounds; small urban

Contact

Kathie Owens
7800 Carters Road
Pascagoula, MS 39581
Voice: 601-588-6875
Fax: 601-938-6531
E-mail: kdoinms@aol.com

Community

These programs demonstrate how community service and student contributions can be important parts of learning:

Community Service Moves to the Heart of Middle School: Georgetown Day School (District of Columbia)

> As students work in the community, they begin to understand the social problems that many citizens face, particularly hunger

Community Agency School Services—CASS: Frederick County Schools (Maryland)

> This is a comprehensive program that brings human service agencies together to address school problems and social problems

The Gauntlet Program: Accepting the Challenge: Lake Taylor Middle (Virginia)

> Community coherence, problem solving, and communication are built among teachers, students, parents, and the public as they work toward school success and social success

Community Service Moves to the Heart of Middle School

Georgetown Day School, Washington, District of Columbia

What makes this large K-12 private school's program unique and novel is the extent to which students make connections with the social problems that many citizens face as well as how the school's curriculum connects with the various aspects of social problems, particularly hunger in America.

The Program's Goals

- ◆ To involve middle grades students in addressing the problems facing many of the less-fortunate people in the community.

- ◆ To build a sense of altruism in middle school students.

- ◆ To engage students in a curriculum that is derived partially from social problems.

- ◆ To involve students in meaningful, significant community service.

How the Program Works

- ◆ All students in the sixth- to eighth-grade portion of the school are involved. In the sixth grade, students are engaged in an interdisciplinary study of food and hunger, and visit and work on a farm, work in a food kitchen, prepare dinner once a month for a women's shelter, run food drives, and sort food at a local food bank.

- ◆ In the seventh and eighth grades, students volunteer twice a month at ten different sites around the community, including food kitchens, preschools, daycare centers, museums, and elementary schools.

- ◆ A full-time staff member manages and coordinates all of the activities for the middle school students and provides guidance and community outreach services. The staff member also coordinates all of the transportation necessary for the students to complete their community service activities.

How the Program is Funded and How Much It Costs

♦ Outside of the full-time staff person and transportation costs, no other budgetary items are needed.

Things to Consider

♦ All of the staff and the parents need to understand the importance of the program and its connection with schooling. In addition to managing the program, the staff person in charge of the program must constantly communicate with the teachers, administrators, and parents regarding the program and its benefits.

♦ The full-time staff person should have a great deal of knowledge about the community and its needs, and work at building good community relationships that support the program.

♦ Given the complexity of the program, attention to detail is extremely important. Much attention should be paid to making the program run as smoothly as possible.

Current Progress and Results

♦ Students have shown a much greater understanding of complex social issues;

♦ Students are demonstrating the value and importance of an altruistic attitude;

♦ Students have demonstrated improved self-esteem;

♦ Students and teachers have indicated how the program reinforces and enriches the academic portion of school and learning;

♦ Strong links between the school and community have been forged;

♦ Students have demonstrated a deeper awareness of the difficulties faced by many people outside of the students' middle class culture.

School and Demographic Information

Georgetown Day School
4530 MacArthur Blvd. NW
Washington, DC 20012

♦ 1,000+ students, pre-K-12; 200 teachers; 80% white; middle- and upperclass; large urban

Contact

Elsa Newmyer
4530 MacArthur Blvd. NW
Washington, DC 20012
Voice: 202-333-7727
Fax: 202-338-0480
E-mail: enewmyer@gds.org
Home page: www.gds.org

Community Agency School Services—CASS

Frederick County Public Schools, Frederick, Maryland

This comprehensive program is unique in the way it brings together human services agencies to address the at-risk cycle of academic failure, children's health problems, homelessness, teenage pregnancy, and unemployment. The model fits well with the philosophy that guides middle schools; that is, success depends largely on the teamwork and collaborative commitment found in the program.

The Program's Goals

♦ To facilitate interagency collaboration and cooperation among Frederick County's public schools, private and public agencies, communities, and families.

♦ To provide integrated, coordinated, family-focused case management services to families of children who are in situations that place children in at-risk situations.

♦ To emphasize prevention and early intervention in an effort to break the cycle of poverty that leads to academic failure, chronic health problems, homelessness, teenage pregnancy, and unemployment.

How the Program Works

♦ In 1990, this program was tested in a small community in the county. The success of the pilot program was immediate and impressive, so the program was expanded to include the county schools and most of the public and private agencies in the county..

♦ The school system, the county health department (mental health, nursing, substance abuse), the department of juvenile justice, the department of social services, and several other public and private agencies make up the CASS program.

♦ The program is designed to meet the needs of the various smaller communities in the county. Each of the seven communities has an interagency coordinator who is responsible for case management and for providing services to the families. Because each community is different, each has a different style and focus for services, which allows for greater flexibility than was previously available.

♦ The interagency coordinator facilitates the processes needed to provide a variety of services to families within each smaller community. Some of the services are:

- Academic support and tutoring;
- Preschool support programs;
- Individual and family counseling and parenting seminars;
- Substance abuse counseling and assistance;
- In-home support for medical or other needs;
- Family and child recreational programs;
- Summer camps for children.

How the Program is Funded and How Much It Costs

♦ Each agency provides in-kind support in the program. The Frederick County health department, for example, establishes clinics in each of the CASS facilities and pays for substance abuse counseling in each of the high schools. The department of social service provides a social worker and a parent aide for each of the CASS Programs, and the department of juvenile justice has established counseling programs for students who have been involved in criminal activity. The school system pays the salaries of the CASS coordinators (about $40,000 each). The county government adds about $1.00 per child (34,000 children), which is divided by the seven CASS programs. Monies are also donated by private agencies and individuals. It might appear to be a costly program, but the benefits far outweigh the costs, especially when considering the size of the school district.

Things to Consider

♦ Gaining a spirit of cooperation and collaboration among competing agencies can be difficult. Agencies and individuals must set aside turf issues.

- The coordinators are the key persons and are responsible for maintaining and building interagency cooperation and can often get support to families in a much more timely fashion than was once possible.

Current Progress and Results

- In the six years since its inception, the program has seen many successes in terms of measurable outcomes such as increasing student attendance in school, a decreasing number of discipline referrals, increasing test scores and students' grades, and other indicators of achievement. The program has seen dramatic improvements in many cases and less dramatic in others, but the trend is toward consistent improvement in all of these areas.

- Individual documentation of teacher and administrator observations indicate continued improvement.

- It must be remembered that these types of programs attempt to address social problems that have been in place for many years, and the results of a program such as this may not be seen for some time; therefore, longitudinal tracking and monitoring of families who have had assistance through CASS are being conducted.

School and Demographic Information

Frederick County Public Schools
7516 Hayward Road
Frederick, MD 21702

- 34,000 students; 2,300+ professional staff; 88% white; varied socioeconomic levels; suburban

Contact

David W. Markoe
7516 Hayward Road
Frederick, MD 21702
Voice: 301-694-1442
Fax: 301-696-0415

The Gauntlet Program: Accepting the Challenge

Lake Taylor Middle School, Norfolk, Virginia

This program challenges teachers, students, parents, and the community to work together for success in academic and social arenas. The program uses two overnight retreats, one in the fall and a second in the spring. The school weaves together academics, community building and social skills, team-building, and conflict resolution into a synergistic and workable endeavor.

The Program's Goals

- To provide an enriching academic experience for middle school children that challenges them mentally and physically, through team-building for the entire family, entrepreneurial systems for self-sufficiency, and structured discipline.

- To provide out-of-school overnight retreats that weaves together academics, discipline, and team-building in a self-sufficient manner.

How the Program Works

- Lake Taylor consists of ten clusters of teachers in grades six, seven, and eight. In the spring preceding a school year, each cluster chooses whether or not to participate in the program. At the time of this writing, two sixth-grade clusters, one seventh-grade cluster, and one eighth-grade cluster is participating, which represents over 500 students of the 850+-student middle school.

- Each fall, team-building begins with a family dinner. It is common for 300 or more people to attend this dinner. Concurrent with this dinner, the school begins its plan for managing student behavior (discipline) and plans for the fall retreat.

- The first retreat is usually held in October and consists of three days and two nights in a local camp. During the retreat, the curriculum consists of workshops, instruction, and experiences in academic skills, self-discipline, team-building, community living, and conflict resolution. These courses or workshops are developed and carried out by different teaching teams from the school.

♦ These threads or content strands are carried through the school year and include additional work in the area of parent involvement. Children "earn as they learn" in this entrepreneurial program as they work toward maintaining a level of achievement that will allow them to take part in the spring retreat.

♦ The spring retreat is a four-day, three-night trip to the Blue Ridge Mountains, during which students and teachers continue to work on the threads established during the fall and the school year as the students prepare to move to the next grade.

How the Program is Funded and How Much It Costs

♦ The funds for this program come directly from normal school funds; the program is relatively self-sufficient. The average yearly expense for the program is about $30,000.

Things to Consider

♦ The program requires strong teams of teachers who are committed to working and planning together. In addition, it requires teachers who are willing to travel and spend overnights with their students.

♦ The teachers must be willing to work closely with the parents of their students, as the planning required of the teams is best done collaboratively with parents.

Current Progress and Results

♦ Students know that to participate in the program they must pass all of their classes and remain out of trouble throughout the year. The results have been dramatic: there are significantly fewer discipline referrals, and tracking of test scores indicates that the participating students have significantly higher test scores in all areas. The tracking of test scores is continuing as a method for evaluating the effectiveness of the program.

♦ Parent support and involvement have risen significantly, especially because the program requires involvement, but also because parents have become convinced that the program helps their children succeed academically and socially.

♦ As students go on to high school, many of them continue to participate as junior counselors for the retreats.

School and Demographic Information

Lake Taylor Middle School
1380 Kempsville Road
Norfolk, VA 23502

♦ 850 students, grades 6–8; 65 teachers; 70% African American, 22% white, 8% other; 65%+ free/reduced lunch; 30% student homes have less than $15,000 annual income; large urban

Contact

Stephanie Stearns or David Nelson
2213 Willow Oak Circle
Virginia Beach, VA 23451
Voice: 757-412-4041
Fax: 757-412-4033
E-mail: stearns1@bellatlantic.net

5

Middle School Teachers: Novices, Experts, and Development

The best middle school teachers are those who have chosen to teach middle school children, and like it. The best teachers thrive in a middle school atmosphere that is challenging and rewarding; they love working with middle-school age children and helping them grow academically, socially, and emotionally. These teachers also like being around others who feel as they do. These teachers are those that have sound and deep understanding of the nature of this stage of human development; they understand the rapidly changing metabolism and mood swings and why they occur. They know about the social needs of these wonderful children and adapt instruction accordingly. They are keenly aware of the volatility of the young adolescent's emotional state and try to give the support that children in this stage need. These teachers understand how the young mind is changing and growing, and is often at conflict with itself, and they adapt the curriculum, materials, and activities to push these young minds even further. These teachers are aware of the difficulties these young adolescents face when dealing with a culture that is often toxic and frightening, and they are there to help the students make good and moral choices.

Good teachers are not born, they become. As in any profession, there are growth cycles and stages, often accompanied by varying degrees of education and training. The teaching professional is one of the few professions that is relatively unstaged; that is, the new teacher, fresh out of undergraduate schooling, has just about the same rights, responsibilities, authorities, and functions as a board-certified master teacher. This is unfortunate, but given the future shortage of teachers, the situation will probably not change. This is not to say, however, that we are unable to do much about this. New teacher-preparation programs are now in place or being developed that are field-based and modeled on good middle-level teaching. An increasing number of schools of education are developing impressive partnerships with local school districts.

Professional associations that work in middle-level education frequently call for separate and unique training for both teachers and administrators of middle schools, and many universities and teacher-education programs are responding. Imbedded in these new approaches are the ideas that new teachers should work closely with practicing teachers, should be actively involved with curriculum development, should be trained to work with parents and communities, and should begin the process of becoming a life-long, reflective learner. But most important, these new programs place young preservice teachers in schools with real middle school children where they can fully experience them in school settings.

In addition, the need for education and growth does not end with graduation. All teachers, regardless of career stage and experience, need to remain fresh and knowledgeable about the field. New research and information about

233

learning, intelligence, cognition, language development, and other areas of educational importance are constantly being published. New approaches to instruction are constantly being tested, adapted, and adopted. New school improvement and reform strategies seem to appear each year, adding to the depth of what teachers must know in order to properly and effectively carry out their mission. The need for growth and learning never ends.

Professional Development

The professional teacher-development models included in this chapter underscore the fact that teachers are professionals who make thousands of educational decisions each week and who are masters of their craft and their art.

Comprehensive Middle School Mentoring: Stonewall Jackson Middle (Virginia)

> A two-year, comprehensive mentoring program for new-subject teachers or teachers new to the grade or school that uses a formal support group to help both new teachers and mentors

Advance Through Retreat: A Legion of Ideas and Strategies for Staff Retreats: Western Middle (Indiana)

> Two-day, off-campus staff retreats form the basis for extensive school planning, staff development, and problem solving

A School-based Technology Plan for Implementing State Standards: Frost Middle (Virginia)

> This program trains teachers to use technology of various types by first having special education teachers pilot-test application and uses

Comprehensive Middle School Mentoring

Stonewall Jackson Middle School, Mechanicsville, Virginia

In any large middle school, it is often very difficult to help new teachers grow, learn, and develop. Jackson's unique mentoring program is based on consistent contact and assistance throughout a two-year (or more) period and helps teachers new to the school, new to a grade level, or new to a subject area go beyond simply surviving the first few years. One of the most innovative features of this program is the formal support group and professional network that it provides in this large school.

The Program's Goals

- ♦ To provide comprehensive assistance to teachers new to their assignments.

- ♦ To develop competent, effective middle school teachers.

How the Program Works

- ♦ Teachers who are new to the building, new to the profession, or new to their teaching assignments are paired with a veteran teacher prior to the opening of school. New college graduates often expect some form of mentoring that goes beyond orientation and this model meets their expectations and needs.

- ♦ An introductory breakfast provides an orientation to the mentoring program, where expectations are reviewed. Although mentors do not evaluate their protégés, faculty evaluation and assessment procedures are introduced and reviewed.

- ♦ Mentors and protégés observe and visit each other's classes, especially during the first part of the school year. Extensive professional discussions about planning, instruction, curriculum, materials, and assessment take place subsequent to the visits, and these topics are revisited during regular meetings between the teachers.

♦ Mentors and proteges meet regularly throughout the year, both formally and informally, when problems are identified, discussed, and solved.

♦ The mentor/protégé support group meets regularly throughout the year. During these meetings, case studies and personal experiences are examined and discussed. The focus of these meetings is on solving problems and providing collegial support for new teachers.

How the Program is Funded and How Much It Costs

♦ Little additional funding is needed to fund the program; operating and staff development funds are used to pay for refreshments, training materials, case studies, and other meeting expenses. Stipends are not paid to mentors, but recertification credit is given.

Things to Consider

♦ Careful consideration should be given to selecting and pairing mentors and protégés; special consideration should be given to subject area, room location, schedule matching, background, age, common interests, attitudes, and expertise.

♦ Time is a critical component that can often determine the success of a pairing. Time should be set aside for conferencing, training, informal conversations and meetings, and making sure pairs can attend mentor support group activities and meetings.

♦ Attention should also be paid to how sensitive or ethical issues should be handled. That is, early in the mentoring relationship, pairs should consider and decide how such things as confidentiality, complaints, personal issues, and other delicate topics should be handled.

Current Progress and Results

♦ Anecdotal and informal surveys indicated that the two-year relationship between mentors and protégés is significantly more effective in terms of professional growth and development than one year or less.

♦ Mentors, because they are considered "experts" are often left out of professional assistance and growth programs or activities. Mentors in this program indicated that they have experienced a great deal of professional growth as a result of their relationships with their protégés and the professional communication that takes place within the mentor support group.

School and Demographic Information

Stonewall Jackson Middle School
8021 Lee-Davis Road
Mechanicsville, VA 23111

♦ 1200+ students, grades 6–8; 90 teachers; 92% white; middle-class; suburban

Contact

W.A. Valentino or Joni Pritchard
8021 Lee-Davis Road
Mechanicsville, VA 23111
Voice: 804-730-3307
Fax: 804-730-3231
E-mail: wvalenti@hanover.k12.va.us *or* jpritcha@hanover.k12.va.us
School home page: www.hanover.k12.va.us/sjms/sjmindex.html

Advance Through Retreat: A Legion of Ideas and Strategies for Staff Retreats

Western Middle School, Russiaville, Indiana

Staff development "retreats" are commonly used mechanisms for staff development and in-service training, but few of these activities seem to have lasting effects. Western Middle School's two-day staff retreat has been especially effective and has had lasting effects on the school. It is unique in that the retreat takes place in a condominium hotel, and all expenses for attendees are paid—a circumstance that is common in the world of business but less so in education.

The Program's Goals

- To give teachers time to create, plan, and initiate new programs.
- To promote innovation and innovative approaches to school improvement.
- To improve existing and ongoing school programs.
- To build and improve team relationships and staff camaraderie.

How the Program Works

- Middle level teachers have ever-increasing demands on their time and yet time is a critical factor in working toward school improvement and building team relationships. During the school year, a two-day retreat is planned; most of the planning is completed by a school committee with one person designated as a logistic planner. The logistics planner organizes the details of the retreat—planning for meeting rooms, arranging food and meals, timing agenda events, communicating with the hotel/condominium, and taking care of special staff needs.

- All staff members—both certified and noncertified teachers and assistants—attend.

- The retreat's focus may change based on staff needs, but the overall goal for the retreat is school improvement, and to have as much teacher input toward school improvement as possible. In the past, retreats have been directed at such school improvement elements as goal-setting, building camaraderie and improving morale, training and education in new methods and strategies, and making changes to curriculum.

- The committee arranges for or requests funding for the event, determines the agenda and topics to be addressed, and sets the goals for the retreat after getting input from the school staff.

- Extensive communication and marketing of the event is completed by the committee; the marketing of the event sets the stage for gaining administrative support, adding excitement and anticipation for the retreat, and helps teachers see the value of the event in terms of their professional needs. The agenda for the retreat is fluid and dynamic; that is, the planning committee receives input and suggestions throughout the year, and the suggestions are discussed at both committee and faculty meetings. The goal of the committee is to have an agenda of topics and activities upon which there is nearly full agreement by all of the staff members.

- The committee develops an evaluation plan that is used extensively to assess the retreat and its effectiveness over the next school year, and that is used as a starting place for the next retreat.

How the Program is Funded and How Much It Costs

- Western has a staff of 40 persons that includes certified and noncertified personnel. The retreat is held at a condominium hotel for two days and one night, and includes all meals and expenses for attendees. Costs for the event have been between $2,000 and $2,500 per retreat.

- Funds to pay for the retreats have come from internal school district funds, grants, and fund-raising.

Things to Consider

- ♦ Schools wishing to implement a successful retreat format should:

  - Start small but try to include as many people as possible in the beginning;

  - Communicate and listen to staff suggestions and comments;

  - Build an agenda that reflects as near a consensus as possible; use planning sheets, input forms, and other ways to gain information throughout the planning period;

  - Plan for potential problems so as to make the retreat more pleasant for all;

  - Have a single person manage logistics for the retreat, and rotate this responsibility each year;

  - Make activities for the retreat fun—laughter should be a big part of the event;

  - Be cautious and proactive with respect to the hotel—double-check events, room assignments, food arrangements, and so forth.

  - Retreats can be expensive and fund-raising may be necessary;

  - Have good evaluation information on which to base retreat goals;

  - Assure administrators and others that the retreat is needed and can be an effective mechanism for school improvement.

Current Progress and Results

- ♦ Camaraderie, staff morale, and school spirit are higher than ever.

- ♦ New programs planned at the retreat have experienced few implementation problems as most of the implementation takes place subsequent to the retreat but prior to school starting.

- ♦ Existing program evaluations and revisions have taken place during the retreat, primarily because the retreat provides noninterrupted time to address program needs.

- ♦ In 1997, all staff members participated fully in the retreat.

School and Demographic Information

Western Middle School
2500 South 600 West
Russiaville, IN 46979

♦ 540 students, grades 6–8; 40+ professional staff; 97% white; middle class; small town, suburban and rural

Contact

Claudia Schlagenhauf
2500 South 600 West
Russiaville, IN 46979
Voice: 765-883-5566
Fax: 765-883-4531
E-mail: cschlag@ci01.western.k12.in.us
School home page: www.ci01.western.k12.in.us

A School-Based Technology Plan for Implementing State Standards

Frost Middle School, Fairfax, Virginia

As many schools struggle with various state demands and legislation of standards for technology, this middle school's innovative plans and programs for addressing these needs are based on identified teacher needs and the use of special education teachers to experiment with technology and instructional strategies before trying them in regular classrooms.

The Program's Goals

♦ Provide teacher-centered staff development in order to meet state-mandated requirements for technology proficiencies for student and teachers.

How the Program Works

♦ Each instructional team or unit identifies individual teacher's technology skills and training needs, especially as these needs relate to the state-mandated proficiencies. In addition, these skills are linked to student technology objectives and learning goals.

♦ Training is provided in two major ways: First, if the identified needs are widespread, the school sponsors and holds training sessions for these needs. Second, as instructional units and teams identify an individual teacher's needs, ideas for using technology applications, or instructional strategies, special education teachers linked to each unit "try on" and test the applications and uses. If successful or worthwhile, all of the teachers on the team are trained by their own teammates—thus a "teacher-to-teacher" process is established that is very effective.

♦ As more and more teachers are trained and begin to implement various applications, the "teacher-to-teacher" model is used across instructional boundaries.

How the Program is Funded and How Much It Costs

♦ By using this "teacher-to-teacher" model, little additional technology funds (beyond normal school allocations and budgeted amounts) are needed. Some additional funds were gathered through school fund-raising events, most of which were used to purchase additional classroom software applications.

♦ An additional staff member (technology teacher) is partially released to coordinate and manage the activities.

Things to Consider

♦ There will be some resistance to change, especially from teachers unfamiliar with technology and technological applications. However, because this program is a bottom-up approach to meeting top-down demands, resistance is diminished. Also, most teachers are willing to try new strategies, especially after a teammate has evaluated the worth of a new technique.

♦ The technology teacher is vital to the program's success, especially if the skills and proficiencies are mandated by the state. This teacher coordinates staff development, introduces new applications, and manages the paperwork demands for the process.

♦ The more teachers become proficient in the use of technology and technological applications, the higher the demand for equipment. It is wise to plan for these budgetary demands as the process becomes more and more successful.

Current Progress and Results

♦ Each instructional unit and team has a comprehensive plan to meet not only teacher proficiencies, but state-mandated student goals as well. Because this program is relatively new, no formal evaluation results are available, but it appears that the use of the "teacher-to-teacher" model will result in improved skills for teachers and higher levels of achievement for students, especially because many of the applications and uses get a trial run in smaller special education classes.

♦ There has already been a demand for additional equipment and software as teachers and students become more comfortable with technological applications and uses.

School and Demographic Information

Frost Middle School
4101 Pickett Road
Fairfax, VA 22032

♦ 920 students, grades 7–8; 75 staff; 80% white; middle class; suburban

Contact

Margaret Boice
6116 Sandstone Court
Clifton, VA 20124
Voice: 703-503-2600 or 702-378-8770
Fax: 703-503-2697
E-mail: mboice@mnsinc.com
School home page: http://www.fcps.k12.va.us/frostms/